Seasons and Reasons

A Parent's Guide to Cultivating Great Kids

I0169925

Seasons and Reasons

A Parent's Guide to Cultivating Great Kids

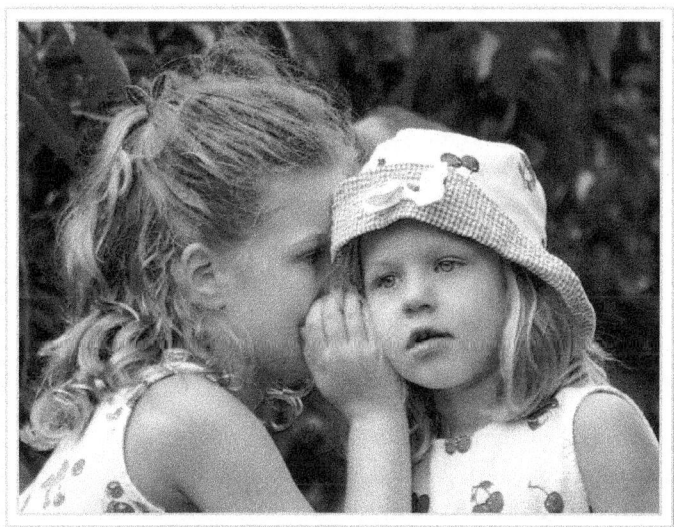

Debra E. Ross

Photos by Carol White Llewellyn,
Honey DeLapa, Debra E. Ross and Friends

KidsOutAndAbout.com ~ Rochester, NY

Copyright 2015 © KidsOutAndAbout.com
First Edition published 2015
by KidsOutAndAbout.com, Rochester, NY

All rights reserved.
Published in the United States by KidsOutAndAbout.com
Printed in the United States

ISBN 978-0-9909151-0-2 (trade paper)
eBook ISBN 978-0-9909151-1-9

Library of Congress Number: 2015931401

Colophon
Designed by Carol White Llewellyn using Adobe® InDesign.®.

The typeface Georgia is used for the body text and Fertigo Pro is used for titles. Georgia is a serif typeface designed in 1993 by Matthew Carter for the Microsoft Corporation. Fertigo Pro was designed by Jos Buivenga as one of the fonts available in his exljbris font foundry.

All photos were edited with Corel PaintShop Photo Pro.
The photos within the book have an art media effect applied.

The photos on the cover and Debra Ross' family photos on page iii, vii and the back cover were taken by Honey DeLapa, whose work can be found at www.delapaphoto.com.
All photos with no byline were taken by Carol White Llewellyn, whose work can be found at CommuniVisionStudio.com.
All interior photos were originally in color and converted to black and white for publication in this book.

To my history professor, Alan Kors, whose most important lessons didn't affect my GPA.

~ Debra E. Ross

To my husband, who has been my companion, mentor and accomplice on this amazing journey called parenting, and to the best daughters in the whole, entire universe.

~ Carol White Llewellyn

Introduction

"Samantha, tell Deb the family motto," my history professor said to his daughter one Sunday in 1989. Alan and his wife, Erika, were hosting one of their regular casual brunches for his undergraduate students. Alan, Samantha, and I were chatting in their kitchen.

"Oh, Dad," she protested. "Do I have to?"

"She needs to hear it," he said.

I asked Samantha what the Kors family motto was. She sighed dramatically in the way 13-year-old girls do, and replied, "Don't take crap."

(The actual motto is a little... earthier. But you get the idea.)

"Really? That's your family motto? Don't take crap?"

Alan was right. I did need to hear that family motto, partly because I had not been raised by a family inclined to mottos or principles, and partly because age 20 is a perfect time of life to be told it's a good idea to grow a backbone. I'm not saying that my transformation into a don't-take-crap kind of person was instant or magical, but those perfect words spoken at the perfect time rocked my world in ways I could never have predicted.

What made the Kors family different from anyone I had ever seen up-close was not exactly that Alan and Erika had principles; after all, plenty of people do. But they were the first adults I knew personally who had a fully-articulated set of ideas that they had integrated thoroughly into their lives, including their parenting. They had thought hard about what being a family meant to them, how they wanted their kids to grow, thrive, and discover what they loved to do. It sounds trivial now, but they made me realize that I could deliberately choose the kind of parent I wanted to be someday, that I was not simply doomed to repeat the mistakes my parents had made. It was a revelation.

Fast forward 20 years: One New Year's Day a few years ago, I brought my husband and my daughters, Ella and Madison—then about 9 and 11—to visit Alan and Erika for another brunch. By this time, Samantha had become an attorney, and was married with two baby girls of her own. She was still living in eastern Pennsylvania, so she and her family were able to join us. In what ranks easily as one of the most poetic moments of my life, Samantha cornered me in that very same kitchen.

"Your girls are fantastic. They are exactly what I hope mine are like in 10 years. So what's the secret?"

I smiled. "Ask your parents. But then again, you don't really have to, do you? You're Exhibit A."

In class, Alan never told his students what to think. But he sure as heck taught us *how* to think. And along the way, he celebrated each of his students, and his kids, as individuals. He showed us what it meant to have integrity, discipline, and a commitment to excellence. He seemed to be especially proud of us when we disagreed with him, because it meant we were thinking for ourselves. As Alan cultivated us as people in this way, we learned to cultivate our own minds, and grow our own futures. That's why the Ross family culture today looks very different from the Kors family culture of the late '80s. Its foundation is built on similar goals to create a warm, welcoming, fertile environment for kids to thrive, but every family has its own context for just what that means.

Even though the child-as-special-flower metaphor has been done to death, "cultivating" is still the best verb to describe what we do as parents. If you're going to garden, it's important to have a plan, to plant carefully, to fertilize well, to water if it's dry, and weed out the bad influences. But no amount of planning or pruning can guarantee that the tomatoes will be tasty. At some point, it's up to Mother Nature—and, in the case of kids, up to them, themselves.

As much as I'd love to title this book "Sure-Fire Steps to Guaranteed Parenting Success," that's just not realistic. The essays in *Seasons and Reasons* are filled with examples, with stories, with ideas, and with difficult lessons I have learned from others, both as publisher of KidsOutAndAbout.com for the past 14 years, and in my own parenting journey. As with any story, we listen, we learn, we reflect, and then we inegrate and take from the lessons what we can.

So what is your family motto? It's never too late to grow one.

Contents

Summer

Fall

Winter

The Necessary Skill of Time Travel

Before I became a parent, I had no idea how much time travel would be involved.

In some parenting interactions, it's simple to know the right thing to do: The baby spits up: You wipe her face and change her outfit, and plan to burp a little more gently. The preschooler gets a fever and a rash: You call the doctor. The third grader is having trouble with multiplication: You make some flash cards and work with her until she knows up to 12 x 12 = 144.

> *Ask yourself, "Do I want to be the kind of parent who...? Then imagine your child ten or fifteen years into the future.*

But so many other situations require imagination as well as a longer-term perspective. The toddler whines for a toy in the store. It's SO tempting to give her what she wants just to get her to be quiet, isn't it? We've all been there. I suggest time travel instead.

No, not time travel to get away from her, although I know that may be tempting, sometimes. I mean zipping into the future for a moment to ask yourself this question: When she's 15, do I want to have been the creator of the entitled, unpleasant princess who believes whining gets her what she wants? Imagining that creature, making her vivid for a few seconds, can be enough to motivate you to do the right thing now.

The phrase "Do I want to have been the kind of parent who...?" can kick me into doing what is really in my family's long-term interest when fear or laziness threatens to get me down. *Someday*, I hope to look back and see that I was the kind of parent who taught my girls to navigate the world and become independent, confident adults. *Someday*, I hope to look back and see that I was the kind of parent who made sure physical activity was always part of our normal family routine. *Someday*, I hope to look back and see that I was the kind of parent who paid close attention to what my kids were saying rather than blowing them off to focus on work or my cell phone apps. Of course, I don't always succeed—exercise, in particular, is a constant struggle for me. But the time-travel strategy helps.

Especially in the winter, our own four walls feel so comfortable, don't they? And that's fine, sometimes. But jump into the time machine: *Someday*, do you want to have been a parent who exposed your kids to all kinds of great things in the community, expanded their horizons, and gotten them excited about new experiences? I do too!

After all, as much as I love my kids, I don't want them to stay within my four walls forever. I want them to have a full four seasons of memories, experiences, and adventures to look back on, and look forward to. I always think that when you open the door to a new experience, it just might lead to the adventure of a lifetime!

Be the 10%!

I have a young friend who works at a coffee shop. A couple of weeks ago, she remarked that only about 10% of the interactions she has with customers are positively positive. Thirty percent, she estimates, are neutral... which, if I do the math right, leaves 60% of the interactions as negative experiences. By negative, she means that the customers are surly, abrupt, or demanding.

Sixty percent negative! I thought that was unrealistically high. Could it be that my friend is giving out some negative vibe, rather than the other way around? Possibly, although she has always been one of those people who goes the extra mile to be friendly all the time.

In any case, our conversation focused me on the random connections we make all day long when we're out and about: with bank tellers, servers at restaurants, and the guy who recently installed my new brakes. Each of these interactions is an opportunity to make a connection, an opportunity to shake someone's hand or look them in the eye or smile. Even if all you're talking about is how cold it is outside or whether you'd like fries with that, you have the opportunity to share an experience with another human. I have come to think of it in this way: In every interaction, I can choose to make the world a tiny bit better place, make it a slightly worse place, or leave it unchanged. Especially if my friend's percentages are right, I definitely want to be in the 10% of people who are making the world better.

And, more important: Each of these interactions is an opportunity to show our kids how to act in the world. Think about it: Don't your kids watch you interact with people all day long when you're out and about? Each of these seemingly unimportant interactions is an opportunity to show kids that it's important to make connections with others, and how to do it. It's as simple as a smile, eye contact, and an innocuous comment about the weather or football or how cool her nail polish is.

BE THE 10%!

A Polar Vortex Has Frozen My Frontal Cortex

We Americans love our buzz phrases, don't we? "Polar vortex" is the latest. Apparently, during one winter week in 2014, every single state in the country (including Hawaii) saw temperatures below freezing. So of course the pundits weighed in with dramatic tones about "what this means" —and that it couldn't be good. I tune them out.

It's not that I want to be ignorant; rather, I tune them out because I prefer my facts boring and unembellished. The words we hear shape our experience. "Locked." "Gripped." "Vortex." "Shattered." "Brutal." I don't like how they are designed to make us feel powerless in the grip of larger forces. If, instead, we heard words like "energizing," "innovative," and "undaunted," we would have a much different (though less exciting) sense of what extreme cold means to humans in the 21st century. I get why folks in the media do it: They want to grab our attention. They succeed.

The words parents choose can shape a child's attitude toward an experience.

I like these words in my poetry, but not in my news; I prefer to figure out how I feel all by myself. My friend John Enright, who is a Chicago-based playwright and poet, apparently feels the same. During that frigid period, this was his Rhyme of the Day:

> *News of the polar vortex*
> *has frozen my frontal cortex.*

Thinking about my reactions to this imagery made me realize afresh how the words parents choose can shape a child's attitude toward an experience. Let's take my mathematician husband's favorite example: If you use words like "difficult," "confusing," "stressful," and "failure" when you're talking with kids about numbers, measurement, and quantity, you set up psychological obstacles that may block the door to a future career in math and the sciences. Choose words like "friends," "mastery," "tool," and "discovery," and you're setting up a lifelong relationship that can fling those doors open wide and give your child a sense of confidence in his or her ability

5

to understand the world.

"Think before you talk" makes a good New Year's resolution, don't you think? Don't you wish everyone did?

Forever Growing

When I was a young adult, I didn't understand jazz. I considered myself a classical music fan (particularly Copland) AND a rock music fan (particularly Rush). But as for jazz, the little I'd heard of it I considered to be part of my parents' generation, and therefore not "me."

It's a good thing we don't stop maturing at age 30, huh?

When I first had Madison, I used to look at her in my arms and wonder what she was going to accomplish with her life, what talents would bloom, what would light her world on fire. I had so much to show her! Soon, though, I realized a potential problem: Suppose I only expose her to the things that I like. She could be a genius at bagpipes or sculpture or automotive engines...but if I limit her world to MY interests, she might never discover her own passions.

Suppose I only expose my child to the things I like. She might never discover her own passions.

That's when I realized that a big part of parenting is bringing kids "out and about" to ALL SORTS of activities that aren't my thing. We wouldn't just do Beethoven and Springsteen, we'd also have to do opera and rap. We wouldn't just watch baseball, we'd have to do soccer and basketball and, merciful heavens, golf. (Haven't managed that yet, unless miniature golf counts.)

What happened was what you might predict, because each child is an individual: Ella loves Rush, Madison has little use for the band. Madison and David go on long hikes in cold weather, Ella and I would rather stay in and cook. Ella and David watch old slapstick comedies, Madison and I would rather read. Ella currently gets her love of, and talent for, scrapbooking, not from me (goodness knows) but from KidsOutAndAbout.com's VP of Operations, June Santini, who is pleased to have a "daughter" to inherit her passion.

And here's the cool thing: All four of us like jazz. See, when you're open to new experiences with your kids, amazing things can happen. Everything—really, EVERYTHING—is interesting!

Zoned for Discomfort

When is the last time you did something together as a family that was fun, but which originally seemed out of your comfort zone?

I was thinking about this issue after I did a KidsOutAndAbout.com video about Monster Trucks. As regular readers of my newsletters might guess, I have not ordinarily considered myself a Monster Truck kind of gal. But after the Thunder Nationals thundered through our area, I found myself kind of wishing we'd gone. After all, the purpose of getting out and about with your kids is to expose them to activities they have not yet experienced, to teach them about all the great stuff in both the natural world and the products of human creativity. So why NOT Monster Trucks? My girls are used to going to plays and concerts, baseball games, nature hikes, and sledding. It's time to start exposing the whole family to things we haven't ordinarily enjoyed, just for the experience of it. This is going to be our year to try... let's see... soccer, opera, and horse racing. We should go to a local town where they do a cave and underground boat ride. And perhaps we'll visit a haunted jail at Halloween.

What adventure can you introduce your family members to that will push them beyond their traditional comfort zone, and just maybe pique a new interest? Give it 30 seconds of thought at the dinner table tonight, and watch what happens.

Photo: Jon Urtxegi

Stuck on Band-Aids

When I was a junior in high school, I was the president of the science club. Mind you, I was not the president because I was the best candidate. I was the *only* candidate. Everyone else in the science club wanted to make stuff explode or watch cool videos about stuff exploding. So did I. But someone had to be president, and I thought it would look good on my college applications.

I was a lousy president. Here's why: I didn't realize that the essential characteristics of an effective leader were figuring out how to make things happen, and then setting the wheels in motion.

The club thought it might be fun to take a tour of Johnson & Johnson to see how Band-Aids were made. I thought so, too. But I didn't know how to schedule a tour. The information seemed somehow too far away. Crazy, right? All I had to do was pick up the darned phone, call Information to get connected with J&J's customer service line and... ask. But it just didn't occur to me, even though I had lived on the planet for a full 16 years. So the field trip never happened. I wasn't even sophisticated enough to feel bad about it at the time.

> Challenge your children to set ever more interesting, complex, and important goals for themselves.

No one, but no one, would have pegged me as a future entrepreneur back in the '80s. And yet, here I am. And what is even more amazing to me in retrospect is that my business's whole purpose is to remove those same barriers that stymied me as a teenager. When people get connected with great resources in their communities, amazing things can happen: First, information. Then, action. An internet-driven culture knocks down our obstacles to that information.

One of our main jobs as parents is to set our kids up for success by helping them acquire the skills, confidence, and independence they need to make things happen on their own initiative. Tell them that everyone has access to the required information, that they need only look. That sounds obvious, but it was the missing link for me. Show them different ways to find it. Then, celebrate when they make things happen, even very small things. Last, challenge them to set ever more interesting, complex, and important goals for themselves. And as with everything in parenting: Lather, rinse, repeat. Do it as often as necessary, and try not to get frustrated.

After all, they may be late bloomers, just like me.

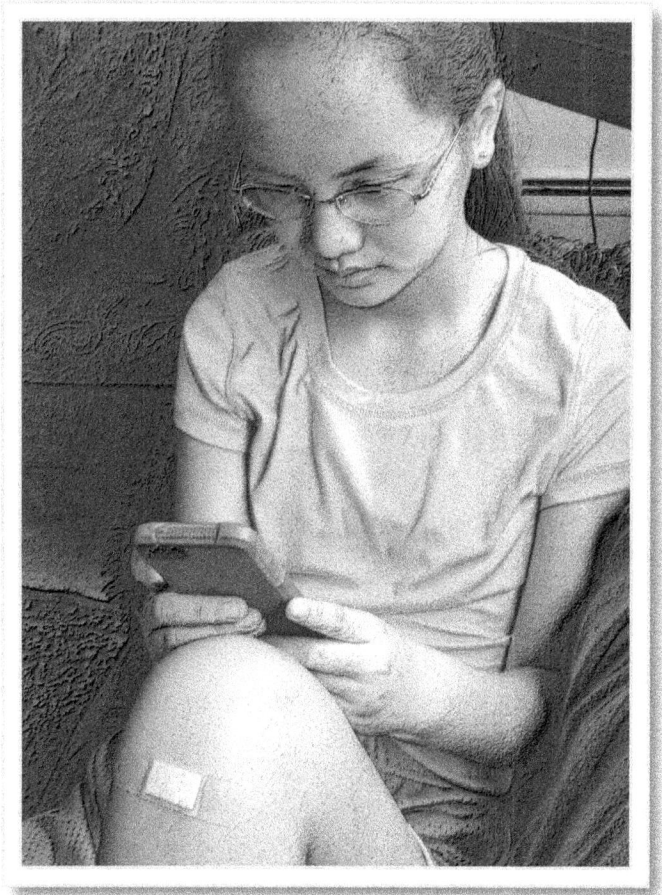

Connecting Kids to Food

I often discuss how parenting is about helping kids draw connections between themselves and the rest of the universe. Recently, in my most commented-on publisher's note ever, I wrote about what it means to our kids as they watch us connect with the humans we interact with randomly in the world. As a follow up, I wrote about the value of helping kids find their own bliss rather than exposing them just to the activities we ourselves like to do.

This week, we're presenting a creative way to connect kids to something else: THEIR FOOD. That's with Community-Supported Agriculture (CSA).

When parents say, "Oh, my kids eat everything that's good for them," I never know whether to admire or be suspicious of them.

Some parents say, "Oh, my kids eat everything that's good for them. I never have to think about it." I never know whether to admire or be suspicious of these people. There are all kinds of good and sensible strategies that work for some parents.... For example, Kelly McCracken from McCracken Farms, a CSA in Brockport, NY has the "No Thank You Bite" rule at her house: Take one bite and if you don't like it, that's okay. Just say "No, thank you." But you do have to take that one bite. Maybe this would have worked for me if I'd been clever enough to try it 10 years ago. Alas, too late.

But over the last several years, I've had a fair amount of success in getting my kids to try new things because I've been bringing more things home, and because they have a greater connection to that food—solely as a result of our subscribing to a couple of CSAs.

Yes, it's CSA time! Well, not HARVEST time, but SIGNUP time! What's great about a CSA for a family is that kids get introduced to lots more types of fruit and/or vegetables than you might otherwise purchase deliberately at a store, not to mention the fact that the produce is fresher, and often a fair bit cheaper. Kids get a sense of what it means for their food to have come from the farm to the table in a way that it's hard to grasp from those (admittedly-beautiful) piles of produce at the grocery store. And even more important to me is interacting with the farmers who actually do the growing. I wouldn't have thought it would make such a difference—how each week, I get to talk with lovely, knowledgeable people about crops and planting cycles and recipes—but it does. It makes my world richer.

So the best advice I can ever give a parent about helping kids connect with the food they eat—or don't eat—is to sign up for a CSA for the upcoming growing season and introduce your family to your community's agricultural delights and local abundance! And cross your fingers.

Experiencing Books from Your Own Childhood

It's fascinating to re-read books that I read when I was my kids' ages, 30 years down the road, I can trace the path to exactly how they helped make me who I am today.

A *Wrinkle in Time* is one; I am pretty sure that I had never considered what it meant to think for myself until I watched Meg Murray struggle to avoid being subsumed by the giant mind of IT. But that was a lesson I never forgot. And as the girls and I have been reading it together in preparation for an upcoming mother-daughter book club discussion, I find phrases and even whole sentences floating back to me through time. Sentences that, I realized, reverberated in my subconscious and helped form who I am today.

A *Wrinkle in Time* helped me become someone who abhors the idea of others making my decisions for me ... someone committed to promoting freedom of conscience and inquiry.

In the article, "Here's What Your Favorite Children's Book Series Says About You," the *Huffington Post* ascribes these characteristics to *Wrinkle in Time* lovers, "You may be a bit of an outcast—a savant, even—due to your esoteric interests. You have a big family, or you wish you did. You root for the underdog, and you definitely believe in magic. Er, science. Yeah, science. "

No question about it: I'm a big fan of the magic of science!

What was your favorite childhood book, and what does it say about you? Share it with your kids today!

Rushing Back In... to Picture Books!

I love reading almost as much as I love writing. But as a young mother, I was so eager to share my love of novels with my kids that I almost made a big mistake.

I adore the places novels can take the imagination, and so does Madison, my older daughter. She has been reading chapter books since she was 6, and by the time she was 7, she would rather have her nose buried in a good thick book than do anything else.

But my younger daughter, Ella, is different: Way beyond the pre-school years, she preferred picture books. (She viewed reading as a tedious chore all the way up to age 12, when a switch seemed to flip.) But in second grade, she was gradually starting to read what I thought of as "real books" and I was pleased. Yay, Ella! Right?

Er, not so fast, Deb.

When Ella was 8, I attended the annual conference of the Society of Children's Book Writer and Illustrators in New York City. At one of the short breakout sessions during the conference, I found myself mistakenly assigned to an illustrator's seminar instead of a writer's seminar. Not wanting to make things difficult for the organizers, I went to that lecture instead of trying to switch.

What great fortune! The session was taught by the art director of a major children's book publisher. She showed us, up-close-and-personal, the careful and creative process of how she works to match the text of an author with the art portfolio of an illustrator. For the first time, I saw how profoundly the people who create books care about art, about having text come to life through art, and about how the art is not somehow a second-class citizen beside the words.

I realized—with some shame—that when I would read picture books with my kids, I would turn the pages much too quickly: Usually, just as soon as I stopped reading the text, I flipped the page. Did I ever give them time to absorb the pictures? Did we ever really study the art? No, to both questions. Often, Ella would point out some visual detail of a book that I had read dozens of times, and it would startle me.

The conference totally changed my view of the importance of picture books in even my older kids' lives.

So when I got home with my newfound insight, it was Picture Book

Week at the Ross house. I piled dozens of books we haven't seen in years on our dining room table. We slowly made our way through the art in our own library.

It turned out that Ella had *always* seen the pictures. But this time, Madison too paid attention to them, and experienced the art as if for the first time. We noticed use of color, the medium (watercolor, acrylic, computer-generated, markers, oils, collage), realistic versus non-realistic art, and, most important, how the art illuminates the text. Our main question now when we read a picture book is: What about this book couldn't we understand if it weren't for the art?

I had always thought that exploring art with my kids would be deeply satisfying, but I had been ignoring the art right under my nose. As a result of our focusing anew, we all came to see this kind of creation on equal footing with the written word: as one more way that humans express the best that is within them.

Photo: Ned Horton, www.HortonGroup.com

A Glass Half-Full of Winter

Am I a glass-half-empty person or a glass-half-full person when I say that we're about halfway through winter? Your guess is as good as mine. One thing I'm sure is that it all depends on your perspective.

I know what you're thinking: WINTER. BEEN THERE, DONE THAT. You've been sledding already. You've done the whole skating thing. You're feeling Blinded by the White. And your kids are feeling that way, too. But the fact is, you CAN make the winter feel, well, winter-fresh. There are lots of things you can do Out and About—most of them free or very low-cost—that can make you look at winter with a whole new attitude. If you catch my drift. (Get it! DRIFT! I just sleigh myself sometimes.)

The key is to do it all over again, as though it were new, to mix it up. Go sledding, but to a different hill. Or go skating, either the free way on a local pond or lake, or at one of the local indoor or outdoor rinks. Find a great place to go snowshoeing or cross-country skiing. Or take the kids skiing close to home. Incorporate bird watching or animal tracking into the outdoor fun! How about trying snowshoeing at night while you check out the stars and constellations? Mark your calendar to take in some of your local winter festivals, which are often free.

Hey, you never know! You might even enjoy your glass half-full of winter even more the second time around!

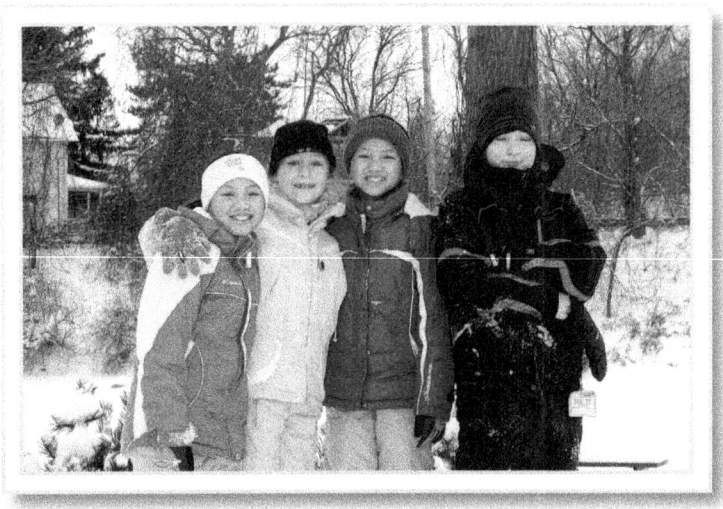

Think Before You Craft

Here's something you can't exactly say to a kid: THINK before you craft.

Those of you with crafty kids know what I mean: For some of them the artistry bug bites as young as 18 months old. Suddenly, it's an explosion of creation. My children even got interested when they were toddlers, in painting *each other*; although that was considerably handier for me when it came to storage, it presented its own cleanup challenges.

Don't get me wrong, I love encouraging creativity. It's just that I sometimes privately wish I could dampen down two things: 1) The rate of art or craft production and 2) The completely-sincere specialness with which every creation is regarded, and which makes it nearly impossible to throw anything away. (Note: I said nearly.)

"Oh, that's lovely," I'll tell my 10-year-old who has just created her third masterpiece of the day. "Now it's time for you to find some place to put it." "But ... but ... I made it for YOU," she'll reply, those big blue-gray eyes gazing up at me completely innocently. I know it's not an attempt to get out of finding an appropriately non-cluttery place for it

> *For some children, the artistry bug bites as young as 18 months old and suddenly, it's an explosion of creativity.*

herself (though sometimes I wonder); she really does love the idea of creating something for her mom. So now I'm stuck with finding that appropriate place for that special something, which better be in plain view for a week or two before I can secret it away to a folder or drawer.

What I hate to admit after about 20 accumulated years of secreting away special somethings to special files is that some of those files are distinctly circular in shape. When I first figured out how to make a terrific craft storage area, I described it in one of my newsletters (for directions, visit "How to Create an Easy and Great-Looking Workspace With Lots of Storage Underneath" (www.kidsoutandabout.com/content/how-create-easy-and-great-looking-workspace-lots-storage-underneath).

It was great because I had empty drawers at last! Those are, of course, empty no longer. And we have 8 years to go before the younger one leaves for college.

I may try my friend Carol's idea that she started when she realized how much she hated discarding her twin daughters' painstakingly-created art work, made especially for her. To alleviate the "pain of parting," she saves the pieces for a while, then photographs her daughters' craft projects and artwork before relegating them to the circular file. Now she has her daughters' works preserved to enjoy, at least two-dimensionally, in perpetuity.

Or hey, maybe you know someone who would love to receive some unique kids artwork in the mail. I could kick in a small bribe if necessary.

Keeping Them Safe

On January 21, 2012, 16-year-old Laura Dekker from the Netherlands became the youngest person ever to circumnavigate the globe single-handedly. This touched me in two seemingly-opposite ways. 1) I LOVE IT when a gutsy young person defies the odds and the nay-sayers to succeed—through hard work, determination, nerve and smarts—at something that seems impossible. I admire the heck out of Laura Dekker. She makes me want to cultivate those same qualities in my own kids. But... 2) My fundamental job as a parent is to prevent my kids from getting, you know, *killed*. I'm the Mama Bear, and MB puts herself in between danger and her cubs, every time, unhesitatingly.

How do we reconcile these two primal impulses? A richly-lived human life necessarily involves risk (albeit much less physical risk than it used to), and the greatest rewards rarely come without some degree of risk. Want to cross Irondequoit Creek balancing on a log? You risk falling in and getting wet. Want to play on the football team? You risk lifelong injury. Want the lead in the school musical? You risk lifelong awkward memories if you flop at the audition. Want an intimate relationship? You risk rejection. Any way you slice it, being able to say "I DID it!" means risking failure along the way.

I worry about how rubber-room our society has become, even just in the decades since I've been a kid. For one thing, we're much more reluctant than our parents were to let our kids play outside without supervision, even though crime and accident statistics do not show it to be more dangerous. "Safe" playgrounds may result in fewer lawsuits, but they also provide many fewer opportunities for risk and rewards, and are therefore less appealing to the young psyche. Even biking to school or to the library, something which was a regular part of our own childhoods, is a thing of the past... and ironically, our hyperconcern for safety has helped create a generation of dirt-averse couch potatoes whose physical inactivity puts them at risk for all kinds of health woes.

So how do we take reasonable precautions to keep our kids safe, without physically or psychologically surrounding them with fuzzy pillows to cushion their every step? I think it means keeping our eyes open for opportunities to encourage them to take age- and ability-appropriate risks, so they can validly reap the rewards. As trite as it sounds, mistakes are better teachers than parents. Rather than preventing our kids from experiencing failure, we instead must show them how to interpret it.

(Caveat: Of course, very young children must be kept completely safe until they gradually start developing an internal compass to let them stretch beyond their current capabilities. You'll know when the time is right to let them pursue their next step of risk-taking, even if that means letting go of the coffee table to take those first steps toward future adventures.)

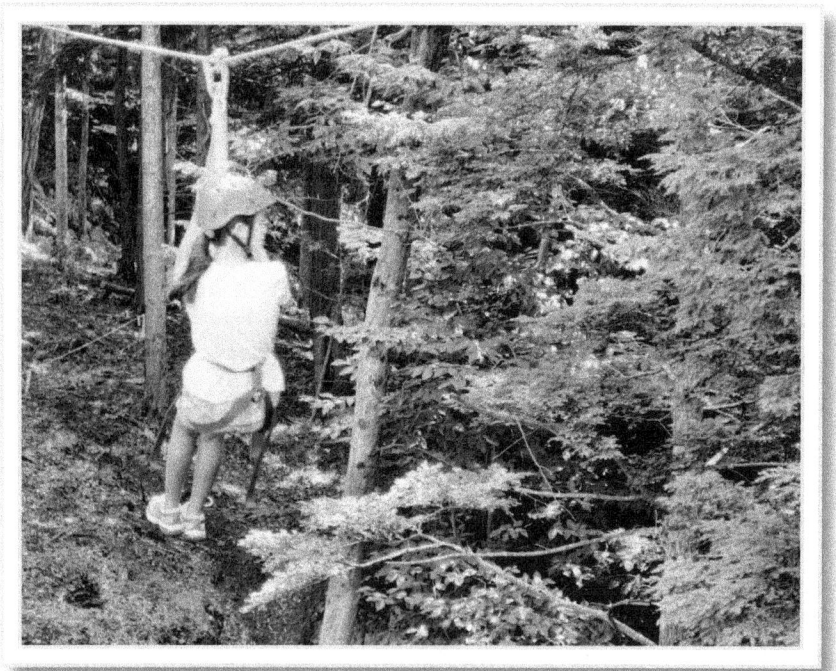

On Failure I: Let Them Cry

The other day, my 10-year-old sat next to me feeling bad over some minor transgression that she had committed in a squabble with her sister. She was embarrassed to have done it, and she told me how awful she felt. "I don't want to feel like this," she said. "How can I stop feeling this way right now?"

My first instinct as a mom was to protect Ella from the negative emotions, to help her stop feeling bad as soon as possible over the fact that she'd failed to do the right thing. But the fact is, those negative emotions are useful! For one thing, they're the logically proper response to having done something wrong; I'd worry about her much more if she didn't care.

Second, those emotions are the perfect consequence: If she actually experiences the remorse, then she's less likely to do the wrong thing in the future. So I decided to give Ella the gift of helping her face her feelings authentically, of supporting her while she worked through her failure instead of trying to protect her from the consequences. That looks simple on the page, but it wasn't an easy parenting moment.

As an entrepreneur, I try and fail, in big and small ways, all the time. You win some, you lose most. How should you feel when you lose? Sad! And then you need to "pick yourself up, dust yourself off, and start all over again"...wiser, this time. Protecting our kids from failure means protecting them from the wisdom that comes from mistakes, which prevents them from taking any risks at all ... which is no way to live.

Unfortunately, schools can't provide safe environments to practice failing, so parents need to give their kids that opportunity separately. Walk that log over the creek, and fall in sometimes. Audition for the community theater production, and work backstage crew when you don't make the cut. Help your kids practice failing small, so that when the time comes to try big and fail big, they know the ropes. And, of course, you'll be there with a fresh change of clothes, some Band-Aids, and a smile.

On Failure 2: Avoiding the Habit

In my last essay, I wrote about the need to allow our children to fail, and learn from failing, rather than simply endlessly assure them they're great. It generated more feedback from readers than I've had in a while; clearly this has been on many parents' minds.

Most readers agreed, but one cautioned that even though the ability to manage failure is indeed something everyone needs to learn, parents must still protect their kids from letting failure become a habit. Her point was that the experience of success is still critical: If a child comes to think of himself as endlessly failing, then this embeds itself in his self-concept and handicaps him for life.

POINT WELL TAKEN! Parenting is an endless balancing act, isn't it: the structuring of our children's experiences so that they can, step by step, become masters of their own destiny, both experiencing success and stretching themselves enough that they occasionally fail. (And we do this all while, if possible, maintaining a sense of humor.)

Whoever thinks it's possible to parent mindlessly is in for a rude awakening, no?

Photo: Lisa Kong

Selling to a Small Person with Free Will

You've been there. So have I. We have this idealized notion of something great for our kids to do, something that would be so fun, so cute, so educational, so enriching, so memorable.

And then ....

They have other ideas.

It takes a little while for a parent to learn to go with the flow. Even when she's as small as my friend's newborn was when she rejected the overtures of the snuggly friend in the photo on the next page, this being is ANOTHER person, with her own mind. With free will.

Ordering small, semi-rational humans to do something doesn't work nearly as well as selling them on the idea.

That was my first major lesson when I had Madison. Before those small people can reason, you have to work with their rhythms, not yours. That is just the way it is, and the more cheerfully you can learn to fit your whole family's rhythms together, the better. Easier said than done, I know.

And even when they start to think on their own (or maybe *especially* when they start to think on their own), they are not actually reasonable. That was when I learned the 132nd major lesson of parenthood: Everything is a sales job. Ordering small semi-rational humans to do something doesn't work nearly as well as selling them on the idea. The goal is to get kids to want to do things that we know are good for them. Notice I didn't say bribing (though I'm not always above that), I said selling. Only one of these is a sales job:

"Drink your milk now, or there's going to be trouble!"

"When you finish your milk, we can head out to the park."

"Isn't it cool how the protein and calcium inside that delicious frosty cup of milk is going to make your bones stronger and help you grow faster?"

Of course, you have to be a little more subtle than I am in this example above, or they'll see right through you (especially after they're about 6 or so). But the key is: If you constantly display your own sincere enthusiasm for something—show them how to revel in the things that are good for them—they will mostly follow your lead. Mostly. My friend's daughter is now 5 years old, and I think she may still have issues with lambs.

Photo: Samantha Harris

Kid-Free Culture

For the last couple of weeks, my family has been racing through life at a flat-out sprint; we didn't even really stop when stomach flu tried to trip us up. So last Saturday morning, when I saw an email come in from our local orchestra, it triggered something strong inside me. I realized I needed a transfusion of Schubert, immediately, and preferably his 9th Symphony. It had to be live. And it had to be KID-FREE.

Yes, you read that right: The Kids Out And About Lady needed a cultural experience WITHOUT the kids.

It's my job—my KidsOutAnd-About.com publisher job—to inspire you to want to take your kids "out and about" to experience worthwhile things in our culture. And when I take my own kids out, whether to a concert, or to a museum, or to a ball game, or to a recreation center, or on a nature trail to listen to birds, I feel great. After all, I'm doing my job—my parent job, that is.

When taking kids out and about to a cultural experience, half a mom's brain is monitoring her kids' reactions. It means that you, the caregiver, can't just relax and enjoy.

But when taking kids out and about to a cultural experience, here's what happens to a mom: Typically, about half her brain is monitoring her kids' reactions, filing away things to point out later, figuring out the connections they might be making. That's part of doing the parenting job right. But it does mean that you, the caregiver, can't just relax and enjoy. It's not the whole experience, it's the Mom Experience.

Saturday, I wanted to use my whole brain instead of just half. So I proposed a Sudden Date Night with my husband, which we do, like, never. (Literally, this was the first time we had a same-day date proposal since Madison arrived on the scene 13 years ago.) We heard Schubert, Mendelssohn, and Dvořák.

And I was right: Without the kids, my whole brain could be tuned in to the orchestra. It felt great to be so absorbed. So great, in fact, that it made me realize that one of the reasons that we expose kids to this wonderful stuff when they're kids is so that when they're adults, they can have the kind of experience I did on Saturday. I think this means that we, the parents, shouldn't deny ourselves this fully adult pleasure.

So now I'm hooked. I'm planning some nature hikes, a Red Wings baseball game, and a Rush concert in June—all solo. You can join me, sure. We can recharge together. But no kids allowed.

Photo: Ted Llewellyn

Puzzling Pleasure

I love puzzles. To me, a thousand-piece jigsaw puzzle represents a thousand opportunities to experience that satisfying little "yes!" you get when you match two pieces together. You mess around for a while with no satisfaction. Everything is disorganized. You start sorting through the confusion and then: Snap. Snap. Snap. You fit the pieces together one by one. Yes. Yes. Yes.

One of the best things about being the mom of toddlers and pre-schoolers is watching those tiny "I did it!" moments that so infuse them with joy. I always relished the toys and life experiences that gave them these opportunities. Those first jigsaw puzzles with four or five pieces do a good job; they provide such a satisfying feeling—even for adults!—when the shapes all slide into their proper places. Watching my kids learn by achieving taught me a

Do some puzzles with your kids, and enjoy the lovely snap, snap, snap of creating order from chaos.

lot: primarily, that crafting a happy life means engineering as many "I did it!" moments as possible. We need to set up the environment, leave them alone to fuss around, and watch what happens. And cheer.

People always say that one can learn a lot about happiness from watching young kids. But what does it actually mean for adults? Watching my girls grow, I realized that I really should be more like them: That is, I should actively seek a sense of joy in my own accomplishments, even though societal norms tell adults to suppress it. I decided that it's perfectly okay for us to celebrate too, as long as it's a private celebration rather than a self-aggrandizing comparison to others.

Those who have been familiar with my writing for a while know my mission has a lot to do with celebrating: mostly, celebrating those in our local regions who provide wonderful opportunities for families. But I think that extends further, into our personal lives. Many of us are guilty of cheering our children's accomplishments but remaining indifferent to our own successes. How about you? I challenge you to take back what you had when you were 3 years old: If you do something good, then take the time to FEEL GOOD about it. Enjoy a private "you go!" zing of pleasure for a little while. Engineer those opportunities for yourself. Not only will it spur you on to the next accomplishment, but you'll pass the glow on to those around you.

Can't figure out where to get started? Do some puzzles with your kids. And enjoy the lovely snap, snap, snap of creating order from chaos.

The Battle of the Coat

"You'll have to pick your battles," the Wise Ones advised us even before we had kids. Well, here's one that will be familiar to almost every parent: The Battle of the Coat.

It's bred deep in our evolutionary heritage as mothers: 35,000 years ago this month, Neanderthal mothers were fruitlessly calling after their Neanderthal children: "Put on an extra mammoth skin, for pity's sake. Doesn't the phrase Ice Age mean anything to you?"

This is one battle we always choose, even though we always lose.

It's as predictable as the weather in Rochester in February: Mother reminds child to put on coat. Child insists it is not cold enough for coat. Mother triumphantly points to thermometer indicating 15 degrees. Child points out that it is only four steps from car to building. Child lunges out door. Mother follows, carrying coat. Child exits car, carrying coat. Checkmate.

35,000 years ago this month, Neanderthal mothers were fruitlessly calling..."Put on an extra mammoth skin, for pity's sake. Doesn't the phrase Ice Age mean anything to you?"

Here is what is at stake for kids:

1. Kids want to elicit a parent's love and concern even as they struggle for independence. In this enterprise, they get both.

2. Kids want to prove they are strong, that they can take discomfort. It doesn't register that we are even more uncomfortable than they are. (And that might actually be seen as a plus.)

3. Winning feels good. A kid can win The Battle of the Coat every time: Even if they initially seem to capitulate, that's just a diversionary tactic; as soon as mom's back is turned, off comes the coat.

We try to reassure ourselves that kids will learn from experience, that if we let them go without the outerwear this time, they'll suffer a little, but next time they'll take the initiative and just put it on. Ha. Kids have conveniently short memories about these sorts of things.

So for those who were hoping for some secret strategy for thwarting the Dark Side in the Battle of the Coat, you'll have to look elsewhere. In the meantime, stay cozy. (I know that *you*, at least, will put on that extra mammoth skin. I feel warmer already.)

Haul That Sled with Your Brain

My daughter Madison was thinking aloud in the car one time: "You know, Mom, 'they' always tell you to 'be yourself.' But the problem with that is that my true self wants to do things like break the arms of people who are mean. I can't actually DO that. So I've got to be way better than my true self."

She had a good point. In large part, becoming mature means learning to suppress those kinds of violent retaliatory urges we all experience, and thinking through the consequences before reacting with vengeance. So yeah, I'm all for Madison restraining herself from sending large swaths of the American population to the hospital with damaged limbs, even if they do deserve it. You go, girl! Thumbs-up for self-control!

But Madison is also making the classic mistake of associating her "true self" with just her emotional side. While her emotions are certainly a very real part of who she is, the part of her that is making the decision to do the rational thing is just as real.

The sooner a child learns to do the hard work of sorting through options to make good decisions – to win the inner war that emotions can wage with reason – the sooner she'll reap the rewards.

Here's a metaphor appropriate to the winter season: Think of reason as the work you need to do to haul the sled up the hill while ignoring the ache in your thighs, and emotion as the ride down after you let go. Feeling is easy and seems natural. Thinking is hard and seems artificial, because you have to ignore the emotions that get in the way.

The sooner a child learns to do the hard work of sorting through options to make good decisions—to win the inner war that emotions can wage with reason—the sooner she'll reap the rewards. Even better, the more practice she gets at thinking, the more her feelings will fall into line... She will find that doing the right thing is actually more satisfying than giving in to flaring emotions. It's not easy, of course; this process takes many years, and some adults never get there at all.

So even though our culture likes to paint a picture of reason as cold and robotic, and emotion as hot and authentic, the fact is that Madison's brain belongs to her just as much as her heart. My insurance company and I are very happy that she is using both.

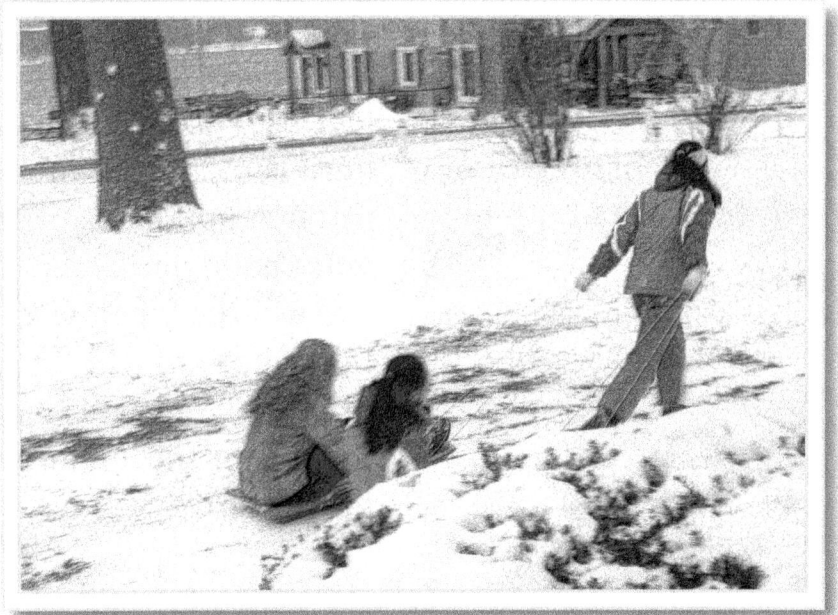

Get in a New Rhythm for Spring: Fiddle!

It's never too late, and always a good idea, to become a fiddler. Fiddling MIGHT involve an actual violin, but really I'm talking about all kinds of activities: Cooking, computer programming, model helicopter building, your new computer setup, piano playing, poetry writing, LEGO creations, language learning, portrait painting, carpentry, math... anything that involves fiddling around to make words or numbers or chemicals or little plastic pieces come together to make something happen.

I believe that the ability to fiddle is one of the keys to success in life. Fiddling requires patience, but it also strengthens it. Fiddling requires imagination, but it also rewards it. Fiddling requires the courage to fail, but over the course of time, those failures are dwarfed by the successes that fiddlers experience. Fiddling teaches us how to manage frustration. It teaches us about long-term goals.

Fiddling also requires TIME. Families seem to have precious little of that nowadays, don't we? But *any* season is the perfect time to encourage kids to be fiddlers. So I try to set aside (for my kids at least) as much unscheduled time as I can. If you have barely-opened craft or science kits from the holidays, put them somewhere enticing, where they can't help but be noticed. Got building toys like K'Nex or a marble run? Even my teens can't help fiddling when I leave these out. Fiddling requires something to fiddle with, although it doesn't have to cost anything. Does your backyard have a pile of sticks? Stones? They make perfect fiddling material. Got some mud? And some old spices? Oh, the spicy mud pies they could make!

The key is to provide the conditions, and then back away. This can be difficult for those of us who see ourselves as involved parents, but remember, we humans need freedom in order to create. Think about it: How much did you ever accomplish when your mom was hovering? Fiddling is a solitary activity: It mostly happens inside your own head. But your kids will be living in that space for the rest of their lives. It's best to help them get comfy there.

Waiting for Spring – Fake It 'Til You Make It

You know how it is when your toddler is busy playing somewhere, and he doesn't want to leave, but it really is time... so you try giving hints, and you pack up the stroller, and you hold open the door, and you coax, and you even get the other kids to coax... but he STILL pretends he hasn't heard you, until you try to force the issue and the tantrum starts...

That's how spring is behaving this year.

Most of our KidsOutAndAbout readers around the country are experiencing a very s-l-o-w start to spring. Even in Houston, the weather is forcing them to wear sweaters and heavy socks. And everyone is whining about it, whining like a toddler who doesn't want to leave his favorite kids' discovery center.

I'm as bad as any of you who are whining about winter hanging around where she is no longer welcome. But just like it's my job as a parent to remove the child cheerfully and calmly when it's time to leave, that's what we're doing here at KidsOutAndAbout: We're bringing spring out into the open, even as she continues to kick and scream.

Just as in so many other things in parenting: We'll fake it until we make it!

Spring

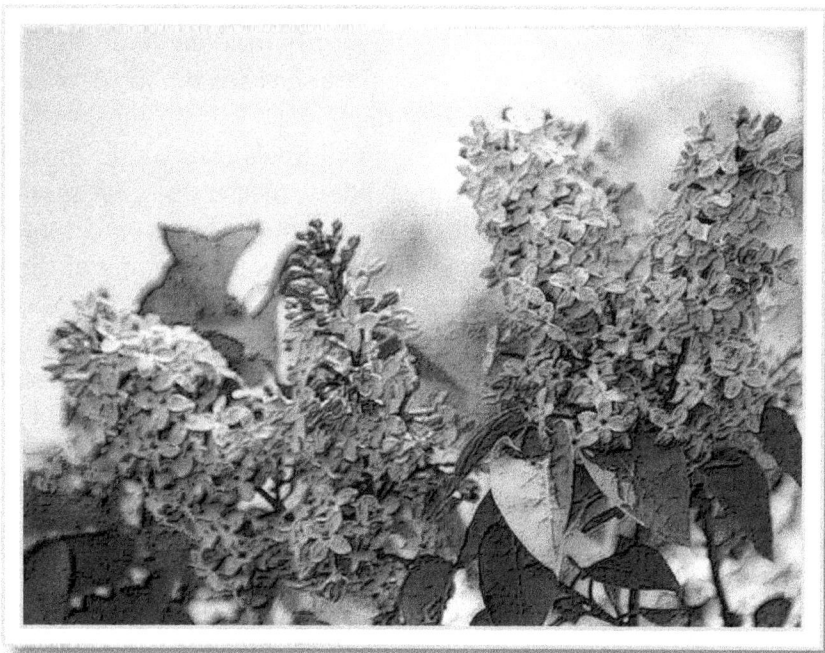

April Is the Cruelest Month

We all know that kids grow really fast: No sooner did I learn to type one-handed while breast feeding than they were angling to go to the mall unsupervised. But I was surprised to note one developmental milestone that emerged quite slowly: my kids' awareness of how the passage of time works.

Although little children have a hard time seeing beyond today, spring helps them understand the passing of time because flowers and plants grow so quickly.

Toddlers and preschoolers live so much in the present. There is nothing like the delight on the face of a 3-year-old, which I attribute to the element of surprise: They lack skill at imagining the future, which makes their present so magical and vivid. This explains why it takes a relatively long time for kids to understand the rhythms of how our seasons progress: Winter, spring, summer, fall. I think Ella was 6 or 7 before she had this fully integrated (she was also at least 4 before she used the word "tomorrow"—she used to call it "the next day").

Fortunately, in our mission as our children's Tour Guide Through Life, teaching the seasons is almost purely pleasurable, because it's so beautifully sensory: Reveling in the seasons engages touch, smell, taste, sight, and hearing. And the cusp of spring is one of those "in-between" times when we can point out the season change practically as it happens, in a condensed time frame that young kids can understand: The snow piles shrink, the days get warmer, birds start singing and building nests, and soon a lovely green shade will begin to creep in. And then the flowers. What toddler doesn't like flowers?

A neat project for April is to take photos of the same place outside each day for 30 days, especially if you can focus on plants such as crocuses, daffodils, and tulips. Print them out or show them on the screen to your youngster and watch the wonder and understanding grow. When Madison was about 5, we chose one tulip as it pushed its way out of the ground, and measured it each day for a month. Along with the day's measurement, we also recorded that day's temperature and whether it rained. That way, she was able to see how the rate of growth corresponded to the weather. She still remembers that experience many years later.

Although little children have a hard time seeing beyond today, spring helps them understand the passing of time because flowers and plants grow so quickly. We moms have only to look at our children growing and blossoming to understand how quickly time passes.

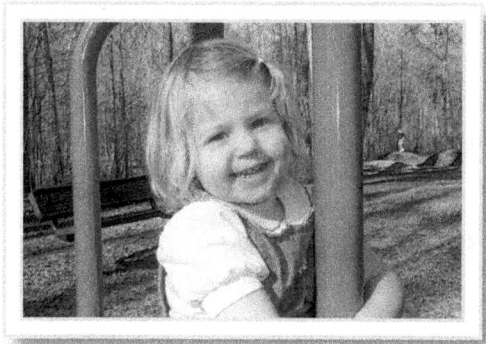

Photo: Debra E. Ross

Spicy Mud Pies

My friend Anne is a quirky genius when it comes to little kids. She had three in quick succession; they are now 2-and-a-half, 4, and 5: two super-active pre-school boys, and a toddler girl who keeps up by hook or by crook. You'd think that Anne would need to stick to the tried-and-true just to get through the day, but no, she always encourages her kids to mix it up a little. She's brave.

The other day, that was literally true. On one of those first truly-warm afternoons, Anne discovered that a bunch of spices in her cabinet were past the expiration date. So she and the kids went outside and mixed up spicy mud pies. You read that right. Imagine warm mud mixed with poultry seasoning, basil, and oregano. The plastic dinosaurs ate better than they have in a while. Anne cautions anyone against creating anything too spicy. Cinnamon=good, cayenne pepper=bad, especially with adventurous toddlers. Serious genius, right? Search Kidsoutandabout.comfor "Spicy mud pies" and you'll find Anne's Spicy Mud Pie Recipe for your early-spring gustatory pleasure.

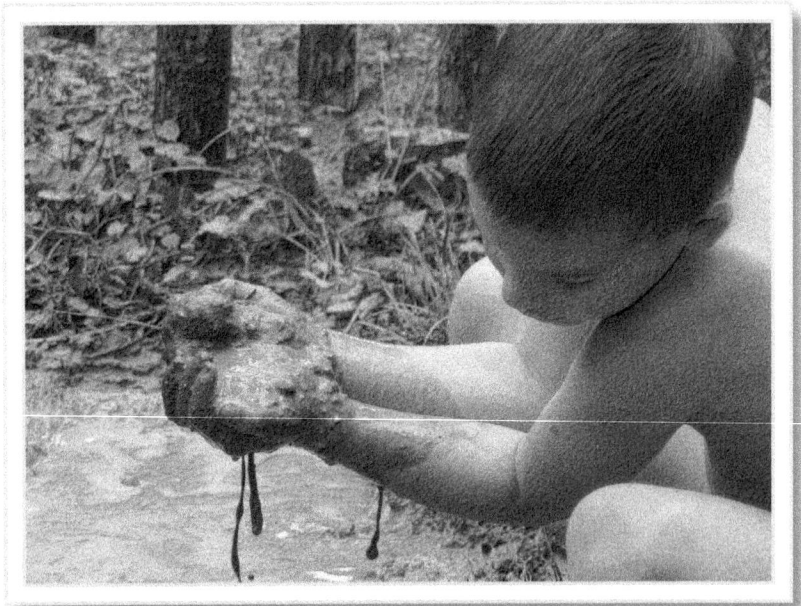

Photo: Nora Pacher

What Bugs Can Teach Us about Parenting

It's spring. You might have noticed it from of the wonderful daylight, green leaves, and lack of snow on the ground. I can tell because of all of the bugs.

I learned a lot about being a parent from bugs. Really.

See, I hate bugs. Yes, yes, I know they're crucial to the food chain, to the very balance of life on this planet as we know it, but I don't care. Sure, it would be great if I were one of those earth-loving mothers who show their kids the glories of science, who make cute little terrariums with real life in it, who don't mind stroking the Madagascar hissing cockroaches at the nature center.

But I am not that kind of parent. I am the opposite of that kind of parent. And that's okay... if I keep it on the down-low. See, I realized pretty early that it does not serve my child's mental health to see her mother freaking out when she spies a creature with more than four legs wandering around her house. Being around kids and bugs at the same time taught me to replace my natural instinct (Getitoutgetitoutgetitoutofhere!!!) with a carefully-constructed calm response: Darling, would you please hand me that newspaper? I'm going to roll it up and beat the living daylights out of that arachnid in the corner.

That skill has served me well as the kids have had new and interesting experiences. If I'd gone purely by instinct, I wouldn't have been able to offer up cheerful phrases like "Here's what the inside of a hospital looks like! Here's what the inside of your SKULL looks like!" when Ella had what we've come to call the Brick-Diving Incident. Some people say that parents who suppress their instinctive emotions like this are not being real. Well, I really want to be someone who is calm and reliable and dependable. It takes practice. Bugs helped.

So, yay for bugs. Yay for spring. And yay for taking your kids Out And About, where they can experience all that spring has to offer.

Teaching Kids to Fail

I've written before about how failure is crucial to an entrepreneurial mentality. I'm not very competitive of a person, but if there is a dimension on which I think it's valuable to compete, it's failure. By the time I'm in my 80s, I want to have failed more than anyone else I know. Because that means that I've done my job creating stuff on this planet.

I want my kids to be happy when they're adults. So I'm doing my best to teach them how to fail.

So how can you teach your children to fail ... responsibly? You teach them to risk stretching themselves in low-stakes situations in which failure does not have permanent repercussions.

Yes, you read that right.

When I was a kid, I was so afraid to fail that I didn't risk anything; I focused only on getting straight A's. Anything less was unacceptable and caused panic. So I stayed on safe ground. I risked nothing. I kept my head down like a good little mouse and ran on the wheel when they told me to. I got lots of A's. But I didn't accomplish much.

It took me a long time to get over the fear of failure, to realize that it's only when we push the limits of our comfort zone that real success becomes possible. Most schools are not safe places to fail. I wish they were. For my family, homeschooling works because, among other things, I want my kids to see that failure is the path to growth: You try and fail and try again and never stop. That's the best way to find out what you really love, to keep growing through your whole life. Nothing ventured, nothing gained.

So how can you teach your kids to fail...responsibly? You teach them to risk stretching themselves in low-stakes situations in which failure does not have permanent repercussions. You encourage them to audition for orchestras that may be just outside their current playing level. You applaud when stretch their own limits. For example, my kids' team came in LAST in their region for Odyssey of the Mind the year they participated. That still stings them, but from the perspective of their whole lives, that failure was probably more valuable to them than first place would have been. Life went on, and successes came their way in other forms.

Writing, if I may point out, is full of failure. I fail hundreds of times in the course of writing just my one 335-word publisher's note every week. I write a sentence. It doesn't express what I'm trying to convey. I erase it. I rephrase. And eventually, I hit the "Send" button, knowing that it's still not perfect. It can always be made better. But if I let myself drown in that, my readers will never get a newsletter.

So, my message to my kids is: Pedal to the metal! Push like hell. You'll never get it all, not even close. You'll almost certainly never arrive where you first aimed. But you'll accomplish a lot along that road. And I'll be your biggest fan forever.

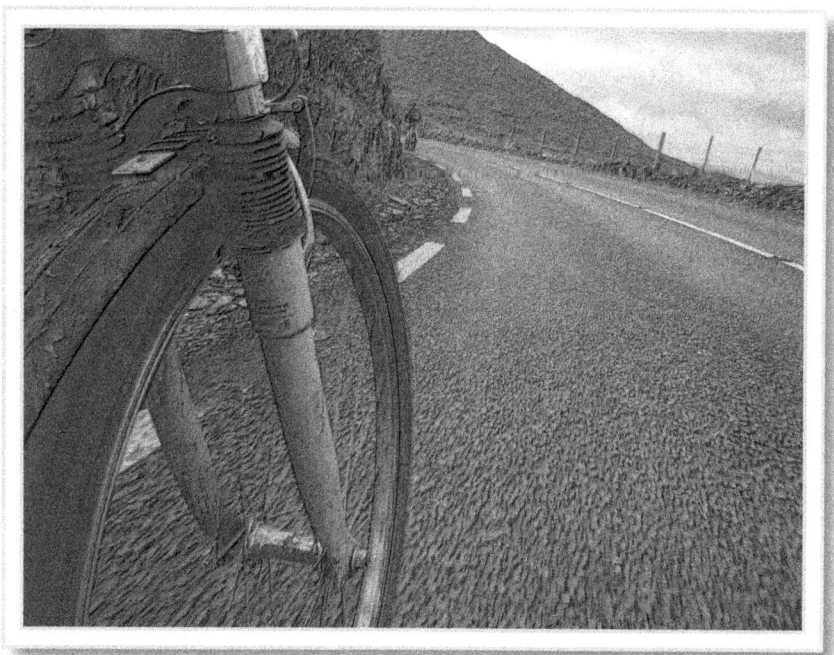

Photo: Nico van Diem

I'm Smarter Than That Star

Most of us have a vacation story from when we were kids. Here is mine:

In the early '80s, my parents took my family on a camping trip to Wyoming. One night, we camped near Cody, a town to the east of Yellowstone that has lots more cattle and horses than trees. Around midnight or so, nature called, so I crawled out of our tent and headed down the "block" to the campground's lavatory. I was 5000 feet high in the mountains, there was no moon, and the biggest sky I had ever seen glowed with thousands of stars right above my head. I forgot I had to "go." I stopped and gazed above, just a kid alone in the vast universe.

Instead of making me feel like an unimportant nobody lost in time and space, the hugeness made me sense possibilities.

I had heard people talk about how stargazing made them see themselves as small and insignificant and nothing relative to the size of the universe. On the one hand, I think this experience did snap me into realizing that my preteen problems were probably less important than I'd thought ... I was only the center of my own universe, not of everyone else's.

But instead of making me feel like an unimportant nobody lost in time and space, the hugeness made me sense possibilities. Here's how it translated into my kid brain: I'm smarter than that star. And that was a powerful realization.

Taking kids out of their normal element and bringing them to a place new for you all to discover together when you're on vacation is a wonderful way to help expand their awareness of the universe around them and their place in it.

What possibility will you give your child on your next family vacation?

Kids Are Inconvenient

Even when they're doing exactly what they're supposed to be doing, kids are often inconvenient. From the first, it never feels convenient to change a diaper, right? Given the choice at the moment, you'd rather your child not be loading one...and yet the alternative indicates a big problem. Your baby learns about gravity as he drops something from the high chair; as you pick it up smiling for the thousandth time, he is also learning that you're trustworthy. Letting preschoolers "help" you cook dinner teaches them an important skill, and also emphasizes how a family must work together to run efficiently, but at the beginning, it's much more work for you than cooking alone.

When your kids get old enough to start pushing the envelope (and your buttons), those can be among the hardest times of all. Over and over again, you have to tell yourself, "It's GOOD for them to be independent, we don't WANT them simply to become compliant sheeple." You say this, sometimes through gritted teeth, from the very first "NO!" of a 1-year-old all the way through the teenage years. Of course, while rebellion is natural, nastiness is unacceptable, but sometimes that's a fine line, especially for teenagers.

When your kids get old enough to start pushing the envelope (and your buttons), those can be among the hardest times of all.

Independence of mind is an important principle in my family; my own kids have heard me tell them to "Think for Yourself" practically since they could talk. So. of all available ironies, my firstborn's method of rebellion has been to be obviously TOO GOOD, to get under my skin in a way that would make me look unreasonable if I complain out loud. This is a true interchange with Madison, at age 13:

Me: You realize your sole form of rebellion is slavish conformity to the strictures of society.

Madison: Don't you think it's better than sneaking out my window or something?

Me: What would you sneak out TO that I wouldn't let you do

43

anyway?

Madison: I know, right? Frustrating. So what is left to push your buttons but slavish conformity to the strictures of society?

At least she admits it! I still think I did the right thing by this particular kid in giving her plenty of latitude even when she craves rules. But now, of course, I have to grin and bear it. I hope the pendulum doesn't swing the other way in the future, but when I propose this idea to adults who know Madison, they say they think Madison is as likely to become a Rebel Without a Cause as I am to start using scare quotes improperly.

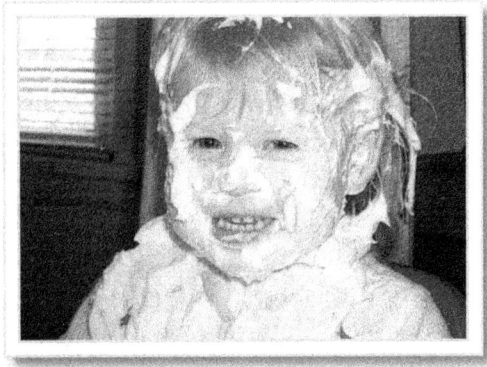

Photo: Debra E. Ross

The Road Back from Stupid

Last week, I was driving on the highway at night when two cars, a maroon one and a white one, came speeding past me. They were playing Chicken: They'd weave in and out between the rest of us, block each other, speed up, and cut each other off to prevent the other guy from taking the lead. "When it's your turn to go, I sure hope you don't take anyone else down with you," I muttered at the two of them as I did my best to navigate out of the line of fire.

Thirty long seconds into the craziness, the white car cut in front of a minivan in the right lane and began speeding away. But instead of chasing him as he'd been doing, the guy in the maroon car did something astonishing: He slowed down, pulled over to the breakdown lane, put on his flashers, and stopped. By the time the guy in the white car could notice, the maroon car was way back, anonymous under cover of darkness. It was over.

My respect for that driver soared. He had changed his mind. Maybe the angel on his shoulder told him: That van could be full of kids. Or maybe he said to himself: I'm 25 years old and THIS is what I think is fun? Or maybe he simply realized: This is stupid. I could just stop and this would be over.

People deserve nothing but respect for switching gears to do the right thing. Kids get that.

The guy in the maroon car probably felt as though his ego was on the line, and it's often like that with parenting, too: It can be hard to stop the bus if you've been the one stepping on the gas during a heated exchange. You trick yourself into thinking that if you admit you've made a mistake, you'll lose the respect of your children. But that's not true: People deserve nothing but respect for switching gears to do the right thing. Kids get that. And what a beautiful lesson it is to show them that any time you realize you're traipsing down the path toward Stupid, you can simply turn on your heel and head in a different direction. Just like that.

As soon as you realize you're wrong, you're right.

Taking Babies Out and About

One of the most common questions we're asked here at KidsOutAndAbout comes from new parents and grandparents who want to know what there is for babies to do out and about.

Keep in mind that every baby is different and will respond to experiences in his or her own way.

Caring for babies can be exhausting. When they're first born, their world consists mostly of you providing for their physical needs. Their explosive cognitive development also depends entirely on you: They can't be independent in their learning and play for quite some time. But their circles of awareness gradually expand to include their home and caregiving settings, then the grocery store, the gym, and the pool. Gradually, they recognize that other people are actually other people, and they are ready for interactive play. When parents head out and about with their babies to help them learn and have fun, these activities tend to fall into four categories:

- Books and story time
- Music
- Active play
- Skill building classes like baby sign language

Keep in mind that every baby is different and will respond to experiences in his or her own way. My own kids were polar opposites when they were babies; even at the age of 1, Madison would never participate in anything until she had first hung back, watched, and thought carefully about whether it was right for her. Ella was my yee-ha! baby; I guess she figured that if everyone else looked like they were having fun, it was good enough for her, and she'd plunge right in. Some babies love stimulation and interacting with new people, others are more reserved. So while of course you're interested in expanding your baby's horizons, you need to keep in mind where she is right now, and then gently bring her to the next step.

Cooking in the Kitchen of Your Imagination

I cook in the kitchen of my imagination. The dream tastes good.

For the past several years, I have imagined how my kitchen will look once we finally redo it: I'll have a stainless steel refrigerator that requires no duct tape, I'll have a gas stove instead of an electric cooktop, and I'll have a dishwasher whose name is not David. Oh, and maybe an island, or at least a peninsula. Yep, it's already vivid in my mind's eye: How sweet it will be when I finally take a sledgehammer to that vile white tile countertop and let some skilled remodelers have at it.

On the flip side, I also imagine being less fortunate than I am: I think about what it would be like to have to haul water from a well instead of just turning on the tap, or to boil that water over an open fire rather than on a 4-burner cooking surface. So my imagination gives me important benefits right now: Gratitude for what I have, and motivation to work hard to make it better.

Parenting books parrot advice that you need to encourage kids to use their imaginations, but they rarely say why it's important or how it will help in life. Here's why: Spring is traditionally when we give ourselves permission to start fresh, to set new goals. Being able to envision those goals is a dramatic leap forward on the path to achieving them.

It's so much easier, and more fun, to be motivated to save for the new kitchen if I can live in it now, just a little, in my imagination. The same is true of other goals: For example, I'm working on a new book. Picturing that book in my hands and envisioning myself turning those future pages is what keeps me off Facebook and in Microsoft Word.

So as you help your family set your upcoming goals, encourage them to live a little in their future success. Enjoy it with them. Revel in your future and theirs—even when there's not yet a success to celebrate. It gives a new twist on the phrase "Live the Dream," doesn't it? But it really works.

What Gives?

What gives? Something has to, sometimes.

I had one of those moments the other week when I realized that the sole purpose of my last trip to BJ's Wholesale Club was to hunt down and drag home to my cave big "food" packages that would fulfill the following criteria:

- Requires no chopping
- Results in no more than a single dirty pot or pan
- Appeals to a reasonable fraction of the family that includes at least one child
- Has a pre-heat-up shelf life that would at least last through Ella's middle school years

The fact is, these days, almost no mom is not busily straining the limits of her time management skills and her sanity.

I'm pretty sure most moms at one time or another have taken this very same shortcut, except for two practically perfect people: My beloved colleague June Santini, who has never let me forget the basil-in-a-tube incident; and Christina LeBeau, who writes the Spoonfed blog. You two (and probably 20,000 other readers) are thinking: That's pathetic, Deb, get a grip. I know, ladies, I know. *Mea culpa.* But hey, don't scorn me too badly: I did allocate myself a special bonus if more than one food group was involved per package. And I bought nothing where cheese was spelled like Cheez.

The fact is, these days, almost no mom is not busily straining the limits of her time management skills and her sanity. Something's got to give. For some of us, it's laundry. For some, it's dusting, or returning library books, or picking fries off the car floor, or that trip to the gym. Or, an á la carte menu of all of these.

Some of these things we can legitimately let slide temporarily. But then there are some things we simply mustn't, and I have to remind myself of this, too. It's easy to get so caught up in the frenzy that we forget to make time for what really is important, like: Listening with our whole mind rather than going through the motions; or pointing out the beautiful art in a picture book rather than whipping through the text to get to the end; or finding active games for the whole family rather than divvying up the electronic gadgets.

What gives in your life?

The Cello with Three Lives

I didn't PLAN to get my 13-year-old a cello for Christmas. Madison only just started playing the cello in November. And she didn't actually need a cello; she was using my perfectly good cello, named Hiawatha, which my parents bought when I was 12 from Mr. Perlmutter, who owned the corner ice cream store in my home town of Cranford, NJ.

But about 10 days before Christmas last year, Madison's cello teacher told me that she knew of a cello in need of a home. Elizabeth said that it was a matter of some urgency for its owner, Jean Vincent-Rapp, who was 92 and ill.

So I investigated at the store where the cello was being sold. It was full of dings and scratches and wonderful character, not like some of those shiny new factory cellos that were going for four times the price. The shiny ones were more popular, the store owner said. He'd been trying to sell this for Jean on consignment for months, and it kept being passed over. But I knew immediately that I'd found Madison's cello...or, rather, that it had found us.

I visited with Jean at her home a day later. I saw immediately that she was engaged, spirited, and not very casual, someone who cared about the deeper meanings of things. Someone, that is, like the adult that Madison is becoming. And I found out what I was buying wasn't just any old cello, but a cello with a story. Jean had bought the instrument in 1952 through an ad in the newspaper when her friend across the street joined an orchestra. The cello was being sold by a serviceman who had served overseas in World War II. Jean had played cello since she was a child, but this was the first one she had owned. She then played it for 40 years with the Brighton Symphony.

If you've sat with someone very ill, you likely know the futility I felt sitting with Jean: You know there is not much you can do, but you want to do something. I had brought a photo and a letter about Madison to leave with Jean, and I told her all about her cello's new owner. We listened together to a piece Madison and I like, Mark O'Connor's "Appalachia Waltz."

I sensed it made Jean happy to be thus connected with the future, even though she wouldn't be there to share it: The instrument that had brought her so much joy was about to bring another lifetime of inspiration to someone worthy of it. She told me how much it meant to her that I'd taken the time to talk. But really, the value was to me, for getting to spend a few quiet hours with Jean in the midst of the holiday commotion. Madison and I are now connected with the past in a way we hadn't been before.

And someday, maybe, some other worthy young musician will

Cancer Capers

An odd title, you may say –

Those words don't mate a bit.

On the other hand, why should they?

While we live, we make our choices;

Mine is the waltz, rather than the dirge.

There are all sorts of dances to take us on

our journey.

Why not choose the joyous over the utter

mournful?

Dance, count your blessings and be as

happy as you can.

The other option would be so nasty, not to

mention pointless.

~ Jean Vincent-Rapp

April 2012

inherit the Cello with Three Lives, and the story will go on. It will still be the serviceman's story and Jean's story, but also Madison's story. And, knowing Madison, there will more dents and marks to help tell the tale.

Jean died just a week into the new year, so she never got to see Madison in person. Madison and I were privileged to attend her memorial service, and there I found out that my first impression of Jean was accurate: This was, indeed, someone worth knowing, even if for only two hours, even if only through the words and stuff she has left behind. She wrote the poem "Cancer Capers" last year after she was diagnosed with terminal cancer. Her granddaughter Kristen Larkin read it at the service, and I have reprinted it on the previous page, with Kristen's permission.

Clearly, Jean Vincent-Rapp understood the power of writing your own story, and as you can see, it's the right one, a message that Madison will hear in her own music every time she picks up her cello: Dance, count your blessings, and be as happy as you can.

So What if You're Bored?

Last week, my 13-year-old daughter approached me with a confession: "You know, I kind of loathe it when you drag us to all of these art museums and things."

The "Out and About" Queen's daughter loathes being dragged to the art museum?!? Oy. It was a bit of a kick in the ego. (For you longtime readers who have suspected that maybe my kids were not just like yours in this regard, now you know.)

Now, give me credit for resisting the urge to argue with Madison right off the bat. I mean, *loathe*? Really? She also claims to loathe having dental instruments

A little boredom spurs creative, active minds.

in her mouth, which seems perfectly reasonable. It felt to me that it would be a little strong to say one loathes a museum, though. (And I have proof that she had a really good time doing a video about the Albright-Knox Gallery in Buffalo. (www.youtube.com/watch?v=nJwHeiO4aeo) But I did want to listen to what she had to say, because if my kid actually hated something legitimately, I probably wouldn't make her do it. (Much.) And of course, if she's not developmentally ready to get at least something out of an experience, it's better saved for later.

It turns out in this context that what Madison means by "loathes" is: "is bored by." And THAT is just ducky with me. Not that I don't work to make my kids' experiences relevant to them... I do my best to connect where they are at that moment to whatever we're looking at or doing. So it's not that I'd prefer that she be bored. But a little boredom is good for the soul. It spurs creative, active minds.

I'm concerned, sometimes, that growing up in this instant-gratification culture makes our kids crave constant stimuli. So being in a place where we can be quiet and plug in our minds is a good thing. Talking with our kids about the stuff we're doing is also a good thing. It's certainly better than handing them an iPhone to entertain them, right?

Using Humor to Sell to Kids

Americans are great at using humor to convey an idea. It's a good selling point, too: Think about hair salons as an example. As an industry, hair salons have the most puns-per-unit (I just made up that metric) of any business out there. Just look in the yellow pages and you'll see names like Shear Ego and Pharaoh's Hairum and W'Hair It's At. It makes me smile before I even head in the door.

Quotation marks started out with the perfectly legitimate use of designating quotations— something someone says...

We're also pretty good at using humor to sell criticism. The editor in me loves the Blog of Unnecessary Quotation Marks (or, as they put it, the "blog" of "unnecessary" quotation marks). The Blog of Unnecessary Quotation Marks is striking a blow for grammar and usage without being whining or negative. Instead, they use humor.

Quotation marks started out with the perfectly legitimate use of designating quotations—something someone says. But then, they somehow came into an additional use, scare quotes, which designate sarcasm; when you use scare quotes around a phrase, it indicates that you mean the opposite of what the words mean. I can go with that use, too, as long as they're used sparingly. But then some folks started using quotation marks for emphasis. Bad, bad, BAD idea! Know why? Because then it looks like you're conveying the opposite of what you actually are trying to say, hilarity ensues, and grammar sticklers point and laugh. For emphasis, instead use underlining, italics, bold, or CAPITALS. Anything but quotation marks!

What does this all mean for parenting? I think we can use humor to sell our kids on the right ways to act, too. You might think you're not a salesperson, but we're all in the business of selling kids gradually on doing what they need to do to grow up happy, healthy, and productive. Humor connects people with each other, and good sales technique is all about human connection.

Want to Raise an Entrepreneur?

The other day, I was talking about leadership with my friend Clint, who manages a mail-order spice company. We were brainstorming ways to help motivate the teens and young adults who work in his warehouse. "There's a clear distinction," he told me, "between people who approach this job simply as a way to get a paycheck and those who take pride in it. The first kind do the minimum possible to get by without getting fired, but the second type of people *own the job.* They're always finding ways to make packing and shipping spices interesting, and to do it as efficiently as possible. No matter what I do, I have trouble finding positive ways to motivate the 'workers,' but with the 'entrepreneurs,' all I have to do is keep finding new stuff to stretch them so they can grow in the company. I think it has to do with how they were brought up."

> *There's a clear distinction between people who approach a job simply as a way to get a paycheck and those who take pride in it.*

It has to do with how they were brought up. Of course, say those words to ME and my mind starts racing. What qualities was Clint talking about? Perseverance, a commitment to working hard, pride in excellence no matter how small the task, seeing the glass as half full, spreading cheer and goodwill amongst a team, being motivated by the big picture, owning one's effort and its results rather than accepting a place as a cog in a machine. If Clint is right that these character traits are better learned as a child rather than instilled by your boss... then I want to help my kids practice these strategies NOW, so that they're second nature by the time they launch themselves in life.

Perseverance. Pride in excellence. Optimism. Big picture focus. Perspective. Self-ownership.

Teach your kids to fish.

Seven Magic Tips for Bringing Your Child to an Art Museum

Art appreciation can be a hard sell for kids, and many grownups, too. Art is old and sometimes weird. Museums are big and quiet. There are rules. It seems anti-kid.

But in 2006, the movie *Night at the Museum* changed the way millions of kids thought about museums: It showed them that every artifact at every museum carries a secret past. A secret past... a mystery... now *that's* interesting! And the genius behind this film is that this is actually true. Of course, in real life, an artifact's secret past doesn't usually involve it coming to life after the humans leave the building. Nevertheless, *Night at the Museum* provides a hook that can make a trip to a museum palatable, even intriguing. The key is to get your kids somehow to own the experience.

Did you know that museum administrators classify patrons as being one of three types? There are studiers, strollers and streakers. Kids are, by nature, streakers.

Museum administrators classify their patrons as one of three types:

Studiers take their time in a museum; they have a specific purpose for being there, and they spend time at each exhibit item to study it.

Strollers are there more for the experience of being there. They browse casually around the exhibits, stopping for a closer look when something strikes their fancy.

Streakers tend to race through a museum quickly, stopping at a display only when they find their attention caught by something startling (or when their teacher makes them). Many are there simply to have had the experience of being at a museum because they think that's what an educated person should do.

Kids are, by nature, streakers, and no experience brings out this tendency more than art museums. We want them to like painting, drawing, photography, sculpture, and the other visual arts. But more often than not, when we take our kids with us to an art museum that is not specifically designed for kids, we find ourselves dealing with small people who just want to get out of the whole experience.

So how can you keep kids engaged once they actually step in the door? What kinds of experiences make them want to come back? The key is to help your children draw connections; to help them tie what they currently know or have experienced in their short lives to the new things they're seeing and feeling now. And to do that, a child must focus. But how do you get kids to focus on ART? It doesn't flash. It doesn't make noise. There are no joysticks or game controllers. In most cases, you're not even allowed to touch it. But art can be fun. And fun helps kids focus. Here are a few simple strategies.

Before even heading out the door, there are several things you can do.

Enjoy art yourself!

Throughout your kids' childhood, display artwork around your home, whether professional or homemade, and talk (frequently!) about your own connections to the art. Convey that each person experiences art differently and appreciates different things. Help your kids realize implicitly that as they grow, art will be important to their experience of life.

I believe that a parent's main job is to be a tour guide for their children on this great adventure called life.

Maybe you say you don't enjoy art. Okay, so even if visual art is not your cup of tea, everyone responds to some kind of art. Search your soul and find what makes your heart sing, and then share it with your kids. Or fake it until it becomes true.

Place art in history.

When my kids were younger, they loved the *Little House* series. So Laura Ingalls Wilder became our historical benchmark for everything. We would say that something happened either before Laura Ingalls' time, after she had died, or while she was alive (1867-1957). When we encountered a particular work of art, we'd do the same thing: Was this around when Laura was alive? Could she have seen it in a museum? Yes, it's a small connector, but a real one. Find your own benchmark and use it frequently!

Prepare for the specific works of art at the museum.

When planning a trip to a museum, spend a few minutes at the museum's web site to discover what artwork will be on display. Choose several pieces to discuss with your child ahead of time. Print out photos of these items, and read out loud about what they're about and why they are meaningful. This helps connect your child to the work ahead of time. When you get to the museum, this tiny connection is dramatically strengthened—naturally, almost magically—when your child encounters the work in person. We did this for our kids and their friends when we visited the Metropolitan Museum of Art in New York City recently.

Life should imitate art.

I mean this literally: See if you can have your kids imitate the artwork, and take their picture (non-flash, probably, depending on museum rules) while they're doing it. If necessary, you may have to do this yourself a few times to get them into the spirit.

Photo: Debra E. Ross

Here, we see Bobby and Ella in front of Emmanuel Leutze's famous *Washington Crossing the Delaware*. Bobby is George Washington and Ella is James Monroe, holding the flag behind Washington.

Hunger for art is great. Hunger for food is not.

There's nothing that causes a kid to streak for the exit quite like hunger. So stock up, folks. Find some way to fuel your young art appreciators. We promised a trip to the Met's beautifully-stocked cafeteria. (It was pricier than your average cafeteria, but that's Manhattan for you.) And we whisked them there at the first sign of blood sugar dropping.

Trust me on this one, folks.

Find your friends in the art!

This magic tip comes to us courtesy of Ella, from our day at the Met. When we were looking at a painting from the late Renaissance, Ella suddenly said, "Hey, that's Angela!" She pointed at one of the elegant ladies in the painting. Well, darned if she wasn't right: The lady's face looked remarkably like her friend Angela's!

Well, after that, it became an exercise for all of the kids to find people they knew in the portraits. They found their friends Ian and Pavel. And they even found one of their teachers, Mrs. Irwin.

How do you get kids to focus on ART? Most of it doesn't flash. There are no joysticks. It's not even usually touchable.

I've never seen anything quite like it for getting kids to look, really look, at art. It was magic. Try it yourself and see.

Let your kids take their own pictures.

Photography is an art. So—assuming photography is permitted in your museum—let your kids be artists themselves while gazing on great art. Encourage them to look through the lens, to "frame" their photos deliberately, to find just the right angle. It will make it theirs, and continue their connections well after the trip.

I love this photo below possibly even more than the rest of those we took of the kids on this trip. Here, the kids are in front of Frederick Church's painting *Heart of the Andes*. They sat here for quite some time, but not because their feet were tired. I love this photo because I caught the moment when Bethany spontaneously decided to snap this image for herself, to take home, on her iPhone. That, to me, says it all. *Heart of the Andes* somehow captured Bethany's heart. And then... it became hers to take home with her. Forever.

Photo: Debra E. Ross

Art Can Kick Us in the Pants

You know those times in life when you've been working extremely hard, but finding it difficult to get traction? When it feels like you're making no progress despite best efforts? When it feels tempting to give up on what you're trying to create and run in another direction? The three guys in the rock band Rush—Geddy Lee, Alex Lifeson, and Neil Peart—must have felt this way for decades, but they never stopped pushing. This power-rock trio has been together for 40 years, and the path to success was a slow one. Until recently, they were ignored or sneered at by the rock-and-roll establishment. But their unyielding quest for excellence combined with the unwavering devotion of their fans (including yours truly) finally won out.

Remember, more is caught than taught.

The night in 2013 when Rush was inducted into the Rock and Roll Hall of Fame, I celebrated. I didn't just celebrate because my guys finally got in. Yes, sure, I love their music…I love it for its complex rhythms and intricate melodies and lyrics that convey something worthwhile about the human condition. But that night, I celebrated their relentless pursuit of excellence…for its own sake, not for the sake of *Rolling Stone* critics. It was a reminder that if you work long enough and hard enough with passion at something worthwhile, you're bound to succeed.

Throughout recorded human history, art has been there to give us spiritual sustenance when we need it. When I was a teen, I found solace in music; this has served me well throughout adulthood, even though Friday Night Videos on ABC are long a thing of the past. My kids reach to the art they love: Currently it's the *Percy Jackson* book series, a few TV shows, and the music of their generation. And some art we share as a family, like Matt Harding's Dancing videos on YouTube and Star Trek DVDs.

What art keeps *you* going, kicks you in the pants when you need it? Is it music, too? Poetry? Dance? Short stories? Movies? The more you show your kids why art matters, the easier they'll find art that is meaningful to them. Remember, more is caught than taught.

No-Drama Pact

I recently heard about a secret agreement some moms made amongst themselves: a no-drama pact.

I first thought about the issue of unnecessary drama about 20 years ago, when a friend was in a car accident that put him in a coma for 5 weeks. That was a terrible time, but it swung me into a permanent change in perspective: Some things are actual problems. Some aren't. Some situations warrant drama, some don't. (Dan is okay now, by the way.)

Some things are actual problems. Some aren't. Some situations warrant drama, some don't.

The moms I heard about had daughters in early elementary school. One of the moms also had a daughter in her teens. She noted how intense the social drama was for her older daughter. And in many cases, the girls who were the worst of the drama queens had parents who heightened the fuss instead of diffusing it: Rather than encourage their kids to shrug off small slights—a criticism from a teacher, an off-hand comment from someone in the social circle—some parents would make a federal case out of the situation. The kids got a lesson in perspective from their parents, but it was the wrong lesson. So this mom came up with the idea of a no-drama pact.

It was simple: She told the others that when conflicts would arise among the kids and her friends, as they inevitably would, she would be part of the solution rather than part of the problem: She promised to inject reason, sobriety, and calm cheerfulness into whatever situation arose, and she would help the kids do the same. The other moms agreed.

I like the idea of a no-drama pact, even if I just make it with myself.

Probably just the fact of having daughters means that I have increased the net drama in the world, at least for a couple of decades. So I suspect the no-drama pact is a good idea. In any case, I hope that I can help Madison and Ella keep an even temperament for the next few years, so that they always can be part of the solution rather than the problem. I don't want them to have to experience the near-loss of a friend to avoid becoming someone who creates problems out of thin air. Will I succeed? I hope so. The world needs more common sense and less drama. Catch me when Madison is on the good side of 18, and I'll have a full report.

Photo: Bobby Shearer

At Least You Remember the Trees

I remember vividly the first school day in June at the end of first grade. "We only have a few weeks of school left," said my teacher. "So what have you learned this year?"

We all looked at her blankly. Not one of us could bring to mind a single thing!

"Don't worry, now you're going to do something you'll really remember," Miss Cook said. And we went outside for a school-wide ceremony at which each class planted a tree to celebrate our nation's Bicentennial.

Miss Cook was on to something there: Some things pass through you as part of your school experience and are gone forever. But there are other things that you LEARN, in school and in life, that are YOURS, forever. Planting that tree in 1976 gave me a connection to our Founding Fathers, and no one can ever take that connection away from me.

Table-Surfing Mad

We Rosses have a family joke that ends with the phrase "table-surfing mad."*

You have these jokes, too; every family does. Your jokes probably don't refer to how NOT to hold a coffee cup, what groundhogs do with baseballs, or Paper Airplanes of Doom. You don't send your kids into spasms of laughter by screeching "No! Not the bank!"

No, your family has your own secret catch phrases; whenever they're said, the whole family gets that little zing of pleasure, because they get the joke. They remind each of us—adults and kids—of our connection to our family's culture.

Cultural literacy—or to put it less fancily, knowing about the important stuff in your world—is like this. The more we help our kids draw connections between themselves and the things in their world, the more opportunities they have to recognize these connections. When we recognize a connection that is mentioned by others around us, we get the joke... that little zing of pleasure.

For instance, if I were to say, "...and they told two friends, and they told two friends, and so on, and so on..." those of you who were watching American TV in the late '70s might get a little burst of happy recognition. The fact that it was a "just a commercial" (find it here on Youtube: www.youtube.com/watch?v=TgDxWNV4wWY&feature=youtu.be) doesn't diminish the pleasure. Cultural literacy is not always about scholarly topics. And if you penetrate a little deeper, you can see the connection between that commercial's message and the social media phenomenon of Facebook and Twitter today. Zing!

So take your kids out and about! Point out things in the world around us! Draw the connections! They'll remember, and next time, they'll get the joke.

*Table-surfing mad refers to how when Ella was a preschooler, she would do the funniest things in the throes of anger. In lieu of a tantrum, she would aim for the startle factor—once, she tore off her clothes and started surfing around on the kitchen table. Hence, "table-surfing mad."

Be the Karma, Part I

When people ask me what KidsOutAndAbout.com does and what makes it different from other online community calendars, I sometimes hesitate before responding. The backbone of the web site is the vibrant local community calendar to which organizations that provide family-friendly activities can post their events for free. But we're a lot more than that: We have reviews, articles, photo essays, many lists of resources, hundreds of summer camps, giveaways, and a scintillating weekly newsletter. What's more, we're real people— just a few of us—whose goal is to bring you information that hasn't been so sanitized by some corporation's legal department that it loses all value.

But what I really WANT to say when people ask what we do that's special is say this: "We're the karma."

Value what is valuable. Reward those who create.

What I mean is that I want to help generate positive consequences for those who create value for families. My goal in life is to create a lot more value for the world than I take from it, and even though I'm not the one creating all of these wonderful opportunities for your families, I still get a glow when I connect you to them. This may sound hokey, but I love celebrating. I want the world to contain more of the kinds of opportunities that our local cultural, recreational, and educational institutions provide. I imagine a generation of kids growing up having had wonderfully enriching experiences that their parents find out about on KidsOutAndAbout. So when I find out about something awesome, I spread the word. I'm the karma.

Of course, one doesn't need an audience of 50,000 newsletter readers to Be the Karma. You can do it too! When you find out about great stuff happening in your community, tell people. (Tell ME, for one!) Value what is valuable. Reward those who create. At the very least, you'll spread this lovely band of positivity that will touch all who touch you. That's the world I want to live in. I'm pretty sure you do, too.

Summer

On Memorial Day

In 1777, before the War for Independence was even half over, John Adams wrote in a letter to his wife Abigail:

"Posterity, you will never know how much it cost the present generation to preserve your freedom. I hope you will make good use of it."

Memorial Day is the perfect occasion to help your kids combine fun with an understanding of that which is most sacred and unique to Americans. How do we help kids understand Memorial Day?

On Memorial Day, we recognize and extend gratitude to those who would give their lives to preserve freedom.

On Memorial Day, we recognize and extend gratitude to those who would give their lives to preserve freedom. When I became a mother, I experienced this afresh, and it became important for me to help the kids experience this tradition in an age-appropriate way. During the parade, I point out the veterans who are marching. Even before my kids had a good sense of the past century of U.S. history, I'd name the wars in which these veterans fought, and mention when that was. Even if they had no sense of what that meant, I wanted them to hear the words:

- World War II (1941-1945)
- Korea (1950-1953)
- Vietnam (1960s-1973)
- Desert Storm (1990-1991)
- Various parts of the Middle East (current).

I point out others who risk their lives to keep us safe, like police officers and fire fighters. I explain to Madison and Ella that these people are particularly deserving of our respect, and that we take off our hats and clap and cheer for them as they go by. And even during other seasons, when we meet someone who has been in the military—or we meet their parents or siblings or spouses—we thank them for their courage. If that is true of you: THANK YOU.

To Daniel Leisner's Mother, Whoever You Are

I have a message for the mother of Daniel Leisner, whoever you are: NICE JOB!

The other day when I went for a walk on my favorite local hiking trail, I was dismayed to see that at the north end of the park, the nice new benches that had been put there recently by the town had been defaced with graffiti. I was sad. And mad. And sad again.

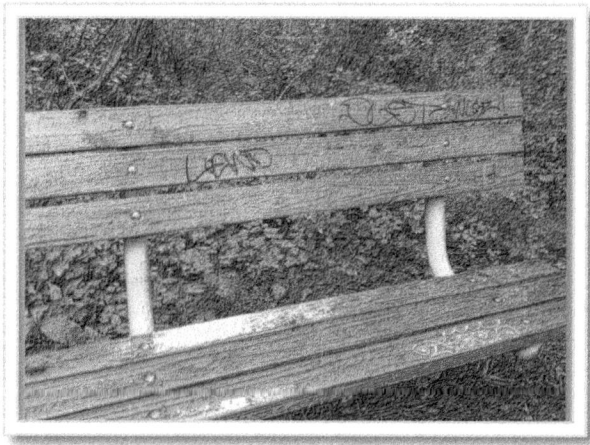

Photo: Debra E. Ross

I trudged down the path, dispirited, thinking that maybe it really is easier to destroy something than to build something. I don't understand it, though. I get that some people take the easy way to a quick rush, but why vandalism—a deliberate act to make the world an uglier place—would give anyone pleasure is beyond me. It scares me, to be honest. I want to live in a world of builders. I'm trying to teach my kids that this is what humans are here to do. At that moment, though, it felt like an uphill battle.

But just 15 minutes later, the south end of the park restored my faith in our future: A soon-to-be-Eagle-Scout named Daniel Leisner (so it said on the sign) had undertaken to make my world a little better: A sticky, muddy section of the trail that has long plagued the hiking boots of locals has a new surface of fresh wood chips, thanks to Daniel and the team he led to make it happen. Here is what I think:

69

I think Daniel Leisner's parents taught him to leave a room—or a park, or any situation—in better condition than it was in when he entered.

I think Daniel Leisner's parents taught him to take pride and pleasure in small accomplishments, and that hard work leads to real rewards.

I think Daniel Leisner's parents taught him to create, rather than destroy.

I don't know Daniel Leisner. But I bet I'd like his mom.

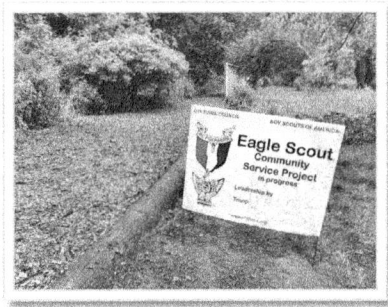

Photo: Debra E. Ross

Woof

Last week's publisher's note described how soon-to-be Eagle Scout Daniel Leisner had coordinated his team to fix my local hiking trail. The response was fantastic: Readers sent me examples of other great projects: of bridges being built, workshops being coordinated, documentaries being produced... all by kids. All pretty much agreed in the power of teaching kids to build rather than destroy. It was immensely uplifting.

I was also reminded—by the actions of my own children, mind you—that even the most engineering-minded of kids do sometimes knock things down, that even exceedingly polite children do sometimes mouth off, that even clear-thinking kids do sometimes behave irrationally. Kids are still new to the world, after all, and they're not born knowing how and why to behave well. A 4-year-old has never been 4 before, a 14-year-old has never been 14 before. As a parent, it's tempting to descend into frustration: "But she did this easily yesterday! Why is she resisting today?" or "She knows she shouldn't push her sister's buttons, why does she do it?" But kids WILL be kids. It takes a while for practice to make them mostly perfect. A LONG while. Characters that are being formed are being formed. Meaning: They're not done yet. Small accomplishments become habits become character.

Frankly, I think it's even an open process for adults, especially those with open minds. Some people hold firmly to the adage that you can't teach an old dog new tricks. Although it is certainly difficult to erase old patterns and start new ones, for the most part I think that's a rationalization. When I was 18 and fled Cranford, NJ for college (not as dramatic as that sounds), I rebuilt myself from the ground up. I did it again in my late 20s and early 30s. This old dog is still growing, still learning. So many mistakes, so many opportunities to change my mind, my style, my business practices, my parenting techniques.

Woof.

Science Is Like a Love Affair with the Universe

Science is an unusual profession: It's like a love affair with the universe.

I occasionally read a blog called "All Creatures Great and Small," by a microbiologist named Mark Martin who teaches at a small university in Washington State. In his post "Graduation, Richard Feynman, and Choosing the Right Career," Martin quotes extensively from one of my favorite scientists, Richard Feynman, whose life seems to have been full of quotable quotes. But I think the best line in that post comes from Martin himself: "[S]cience is an unusual profession: It's like a love affair with the universe."

Popular culture tends to portray science as a stuffy, brainy, remote profession to be left up to geniuses...not to everyday people, and probably not to our kids.

Popular culture tends to portray science as a stuffy, brainy, remote profession to be left up to geniuses...not to everyday people, and probably not to our kids. But that's wrong. Essays like Martin's almost make me wish I had gone into science myself, because I do love that zing of pleasure that comes from working hard and then understanding something new. I live with a scientist, so I know: Martin's quote captures exactly the sense of what it means to a scientist to BE a scientist. I'd like my kids to know this, too.

We want our kids to have a love affair with whatever career they pursue, right? So it makes sense to leave all of their doors open. If we'd like our kids to have the opportunity to have a life filled with discovery, we need to cultivate a joy in learning early on, as well as the attitude that nothing is closed to someone of normal abilities who works hard: If someone can learn it, so can you. Summer is a wonderful time for this, as it provides so many opportunities to learn—with all of our senses, and without stress. In the summer, we can play... play with numbers, play out in nature, play with water, play with building and mixing and combining and tasting and seeing what would happen if....

If our kids see the universe as their friend, that's a precursor to success in all endeavors, not just in science. But hey, friendship might be the first step to love. You never know. So let's fling that door open wide, and put out the welcome mat for summer.

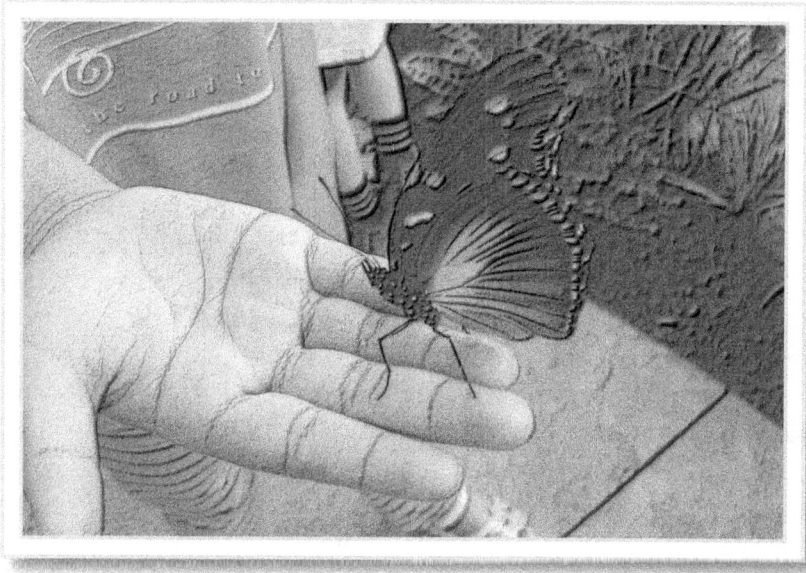

It's All Material

Right around the time I realized that everything is interesting, I also realized that everything is useful...especially the bad stuff. Because it's a story.

When I was 15 and got a 6 (out of 100) on an English quiz because I had neglected to read *Huckleberry Finn*, what I saw as total disaster would instead become an important story about how facing facts honestly and failing can be a prouder moment than getting an A.

Fifteen years later, when Madison was not born on 9/9/99 but at 2:46 AM on 9/10/99 after 21 hours of labor, I comforted myself around midnight by thinking that at least it would make an interesting life-long story of expectation, disappointment, and acceptance. (Of course, that was between contractions. During them, I pretty much just had thoughts that are not printable here.)

When I was camping with my kids one cold, rainy night in the Adirondacks, with nothing between my two little girls and the (imaginary) bears except the nylon tent fabric, I gritted my teeth and vowed that I'd get a lot of mileage out of that story. Especially when the drip-drip-drip of the rain forced me temporarily to abandon Madison and Ella to sprint to the campsite bathroom at 3 AM.

This past weekend, when Mother Nature got busy flinging me into rocks during a river-rapids tubing excursion, I did not comfort myself by thinking what a great story it was going to make... No, what ran through my mind was that I now understood Newton's Second Law of Motion, F=MA (force = mass times acceleration). That, and "AAAAAACKKK!" But NOW, it makes a good story. The scatter chart of bruises on my legs even make useful props.

See, by understanding that everything in your life is part of a story the ending of which YOU get to write, you integrate even your painful life experiences in a way that means something, both to you and to your kids. (And then you get to bore them for years by telling it over and over!)

So the next time that your toddler decides to paint your office chairs with your new scarlet nail polish, remember—as you're trying fruitlessly to scrub it out with acetone—that it's all material.

Listen to That Old Song

This past weekend, I was driving late at night on my way back from a festival when I stopped at a gas station out in the middle of nowhere. I was just hanging up the pump when an old Indigo Girls song, "Least Complicated," came on over the loudspeaker. I thought to myself happily, as one does when encountering a meaningful old song out of the blue, "Wow, what are the chances?"

I got back in the car, turned it on, and started to pull out. But then I somehow felt compelled to stop and roll down the window to listen. For a few moments, I was transported blissfully back to the mid '90s when David and I first got together. Then I told myself, "This is silly. This song is on your iPod on the seat next to you. You have a long way to go tonight. Be a grownup, put in the earbuds, and get on your way."

A good song played on the radio feels WAY more meaningful than one you turn on deliberately.

Most of us have this experience: A good song played on the radio feels WAY more meaningful than one you turn on deliberately. Some even think it's a matter of cosmic coincidence, though my mind doesn't swing that way; I think meaning is what humans make of it. So what did I make of this? I realized that coming unexpectedly upon an old song is like rounding a corner and finding a delightful piece of your own soul floating in the breeze. You have the opportunity to acknowledge it, greet it, and celebrate it.

So I did. I listened all the way through. It was the least complicated thing to do, anyway.

P.S. And this is a promise: The next time that One Direction's "What Makes You Beautiful" comes on the radio and my kids clamor, "Leave it on! We love that song!" even though it plays seventy-gazillion times a day, I'm not going to switch the station.

Seasons and Reasons

Blissful Mediocrity

I'm a mediocre cellist. So mediocre, in fact, that I almost hesitate to say I play cello, especially in my social circles, where even if you yourself aren't married to a professional musician, your best friend is. But I do say it, and I say it proudly: I'm a cellist, though not a good one.

Regular readers of my newsletter know that excellence is high up on the list of values that I hope parents convey to their kids. But being a mediocre musician so far beats being someone who has never studied an instrument that I want to convince all of you to give your kids this opportunity at some point in their childhood.

Playing music is FUN, and NICE PEOPLE are involved. When you're not a viruoso, you have the freedom to create without pressure.

Playing music is MEANING-FUL, even to a kid. A child in her first orchestra, band, or chorus concert has the startling experience of working hard together with others to create art that matters. And as they all get better, it gets even nicer, for both performers and audience.

Playing music is FUN, and NICE PEOPLE are involved. When you're not a virtuoso, you have the freedom to create without pressure. The person sitting in the orchestra next to you is likely there for the same reason you are. And for the most part, they're lovely people, the kind you want to invite out for ice cream after your concert.

The value of playing music lasts FOREVER. When mediocre musicians grow up, they understand other people's musical performances in a way they couldn't had they not studied music. As a kid, this didn't mean much to me, but as an adult, I have realized that I can have a radically richer experience of a concert or a recording than I would have otherwise. It matters. Art matters.

A child who takes music into her hands will take it into her own heart for the rest of her life.

By George, You're Rich!

People made a big fuss over the newly-born royal baby over across the pond. Call me relentlessly plebeian if you like, but I just don't get it. Sure, my own girls went through a princess phase, same as the next red-blooded American preschooler, but that was all about the blingy dress. Some people might envy that new little boy: You're going to be king, your life is set, you never have to worry about money. Right? Well, I don't think so.

I do think that to be happy in life, you have to be rich. Of course, as long-time readers will expect, my definition of rich is somewhat RICHER than the common one that involves mere cash. So here is why I think your kids are likely to grow up richer than Baby George:

Kids need to see their lives as a blank canvas onto which they can paint anything.

Kids need to see their lives as a blank canvas onto which they can paint anything. A script foreordained by your ancestors necessarily limits your options. Suppose the new royal baby someday yearns to be an architect, or a professional violinist, or an actuary, or a web publisher? Sorry, buddy, you're out of luck.

Kids need the freedom to change their roles, their personalities, their interests...without consequence, and without interference. That's what growth IS, and it is a terribly private process. I cannot imagine a more restrictive environment than the public eye.

Those who are truly rich can call their accomplishments their own. There is immense value in the struggle, and its aftermath, to achieve a goal. But you can't bask in the glow of success if the lights have been trained on you since Day One.

So, to those of you who, like me, are oh-so-common and ordinary: Take heart! Your kids will be richer for it.

Ostriches Are Ugly, but They Don't Know It

When my daughter Madison was almost 8 years old, she auditioned for a local children's chorus. She really wanted to get in, so she practiced hard for several weeks. She was very nervous. The day before the audition, she said to me, "I don't want it to be tomorrow. Today is still the day when the bad thing hasn't happened yet."

...The desire to evade reality is a normal human impulse: a sense that if we don't know about the bad thing, it's not really true and we don't have to deal with it.

Here's another version of the same impulse: In 10th grade, I put off looking at my 3rd-quarter report card for 3 weeks because I was afraid of what I'd received in Algebra 2. (It was a B.)

It's so much easier to stick one's head in the sand, isn't it? *If I don't know it, then it's not true.*

You'd think I might have learned something in 30 years, but I experienced the same kind of reaction last week: I pulled out a pair of shorts that I hadn't seen since last summer, a somewhat...er... form-fitting pair. Would they still fit? I didn't know. And if I didn't know, then I wouldn't have to deal with what it meant if they were too tight, right? So I wimped out. I put them back on the shelf.

You've experienced it too; everyone has. I think that the desire to evade reality is a normal human impulse: a sense that if we don't know about the bad thing, it's not really true and we don't have to deal with it. But if simple age and experience don't make us wiser about this, as it clearly hadn't in my case, then what will? Well, thinking about it logically helps. In my case, I imagined confessing about the shorts to Madison, who is now a teenager and would positively relish the opportunity, legitimately, to call me out on my spinelessness.

That did it. I marched back to the closet and got the shorts. Yeah. I have some work to do.

Independence

Tomorrow is Independence Day. It is a day we Americans celebrate freedom, and think about what it means for a country to be free, and what it took to become a country that is free. Today, I'm thinking about what our country's unique dedication to freedom will mean for my daughters, Madison and Ella...not right now, but when they're adults. How can they learn to promote freedom, to defend freedom, and most important, to embrace the joy and fulfillment that freedom makes possible?

Freedom of the marketplace: My girls will be free to create their own means of survival and prosperity. Whether they work for someone else or become their own boss, a successful career in the 21st century will require entrepreneurial skills. So we cultivate initiative, creativity, persistence, and leadership.

Freedom to explore: We live in a beautiful and, sometimes, not-so-beautiful country. Traveling through it to learn about all different kinds of people and landscapes and ways of life will enrich my daughters in ways they can't even imagine. So we cultivate a spirit of adventure, of curiosity, of interest in everything around them.

Freedom of expression: The First Amendment to the Constitution affirms our right to express ideas free of government restraint. As we're all aware, this protects the expression of many foolish, ugly, vicious ideas, even as it protects the ideas that are the highest purpose of free speech: ideas with powerful potential for benevolent change. What my girls express someday needs to be well-thought-through, so we cultivate the habits of reason, careful listening, and respect for the facts.

What do all of these qualities—initiative, leadership, creativity, curiosity, reason, and the rest—add up to? Well, what do you know: They are all different faces of the same concept: INDEPENDENCE.

Happy Independence Day.

Nothing Is Boring

Every year at this time, our thoughts turn to school.

Unfortunately, though I did fine in school, my impression of what I was doing there was less than positive. So mid-August was usually filled with dread as I contemplated another year of what I thought of as imprisonment. It took me a long time after I left school to talk myself back into loving learning.

"Once that passion for learning is discovered, learning becomes its own reward.

As an adult, I have thought about ways that adults might have helped me enjoy those years more, to retain more of what I learned, and to look forward to the day after Labor Day. The most significant thing someone could have done, I think, would have been to have shown an actual interest in what I was learning. Sounds simple, right? Some of my teachers clearly did have that passion for their subjects, and did their best to ignite it in their students. But it would have made a real difference if an adult close to me had shown me that what I was learning was part of his or her world, the adult world, my world, and that learning will make one happy. I can imagine how different those years would have been if the adults I knew had been able joyfully to connect the multiplication tables, the exports of Peru, the Sphinx, the subjunctive tense, with stuff I cared about, with stuff they cared about.

What I didn't know then, that I know now, is that NO information is boring when properly presented. I can create my own joy and connectedness now, but I couldn't then. So that is the gift that I am trying to give my own kids; and I have found that going "out and about" with them makes it even easier for us all to keep learning together.

And once that passion for learning is discovered, learning becomes its own reward.

Wet Blankets for Everyone! When They Hate What You Love

For many years before I had kids, I thought hard about the kind of parent I wanted to be. Back in the '70s, when child psychology was in its ascendance, I'd often read my mother's advice books before she got to them. I remember telling her when I was 10 or so, in response to a technique she was trying: "That's fogging, Mom. It's from *When I Say No, I Feel Guilty*. It won't work on me." I vowed to do things differently than my parents did, and it has actually worked out that way. Thinking through childrearing in advance—not popular during our parents' generation, where one mostly had kids just because that's what people did—really works.

But there were many aspects of parenting that I wasn't prepared for. One of those was how it would feel when my kids hated something I loved. They don't talk about THAT in advice books! For example: This time of year we are awash in wonderful fruits and vegetables from the CSAs, and my colleague June Santini and I divide our shares each week. The bounty is HUGE nowadays, especially when you get to pick your own, as Ella and I did on Saturday as part of our privileges from Wickham Farms.

> *There were many aspects of parenting that I wasn't prepared for. One of those was how it would feel when my kids hated something I loved.*

So my kitchen is filled with the season's bounty and wonderful new things to taste. We've tried kohlrabi and tomatillos and I've roasted my first beets and I've presented my family with a terrific recipe I devised for Swiss chard. I admit to giving away every single eggplant that comes my way, because I have an irrational prejudice against eggplant. For the most part, though, it's wonderful.

But it seems that my children's main job these days is to throw a wet blanket over it all. They meet every new dish with stony suspicion, as though I'm trying to trick them into being tortured rather than presenting them with a gustatory gift. It's hard to take delight in something when your joy is met with a scowl. So I fake it until I feel good about it again. (Fortunately, I have a husband who praises my cooking to the skies, probably in an attempt to trick the kids into mustering some enthusiasm.)

I wish I'd known this, and a thousand other small things, before I had kids.

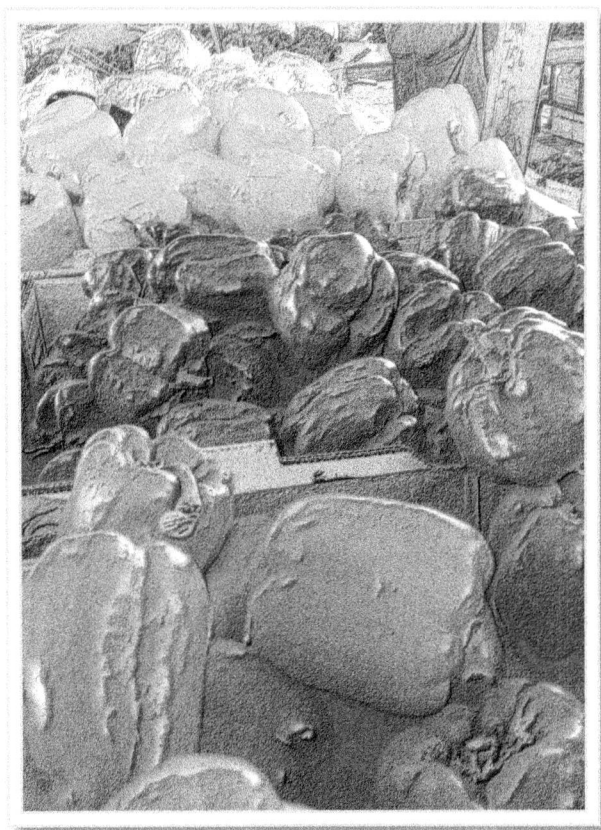

Who Do Our Kids Belong To?

Who do our children belong to?

I know what you're thinking: "Deb, my children belong to ME. They're mine. They're knit inseparably into my soul until the end of time." Believe me, I hear you, and I feel the same way. And that's why this piece tugged at me so profoundly that I'm still thinking about it days later.

Katie Beltramo, our Albany-area KidsOutAndAbout.com editor, is a talented essayist; she runs Capital District Fun in Albany and has a large following. She also gets to write about personally meaningful topics, and her essay, "In the NICU," is about the first days after she gave birth to her oldest daughter. Here's the line that got me: *The nurse again. She waits a beat, then retrieves her baby from my incompetent arms.*

I'm proud to be able to let go as they become more competent, but at the same time, I want to keep them small, to keep them safe, to guide them every step of the way.

Her baby, not Katie's, at least for those days.

As parents, we vibrate with the wrongness of strangers coming between us and our children. Every cell of my body resonates with Katie's story. And it got me thinking: In a certain sense, it's happening to us parents every single day: As they grow, Madison and Ella are less and less mine and more their very own selves. I'm proud to be able to let go as they become more competent, but at the same time, I want to keep them small, to keep them safe, to guide them every step of the way. Nowadays, they make their own mistakes, and have their own successes, and those are not mine. It's all good, and proper, and the way life should go. But it is not always easy to balance living vibrantly in the present while a stranger named The Future is calling our children to a path that is theirs, not ours. The fact that good things do end, though, is what makes them ever more precious while we have them, and I try to cling to that preciousness while acknowledging my own grief about the parenting chapter of my life ending someday.

Who do our children belong to? They belong to themselves, they belong to the future, and yes, they belong to us, forever. Hug those babies, no matter how old they are.

WHOA Can Be Better than GO

KidsOutAndAbout.com readers say to me now and then, "I love reading your newsletter, but sometimes when I do, I feel guilty. There's so much great stuff out there to do with our kids, and I just can't live up to it."

Don't worry. You're not supposed to. As a profound stop sign I saw in Wyoming says:

WHOA.

Look, good parenting isn't about cramming. Feeding, yes, because minds and characters need to be fed regularly to grow. I try to make sure that over the course of my kids' young lives (not over the course of a weekend), they experience and learn about a huge variety of things. Sure, my family's "out and about" life is more varied than the average family's. It's my job, after all, and I'm grateful that my kids are so integral to it. But there are lots of things in the area where I live that I haven't actually done yet, and I've been writing my weekly Kids Out and About newsletter since 2001. I've never been to the Jello Museum in Leroy, NY (though Madison and Ella have). I haven't taken an actual tour at the Susan B. Anthony House in Rochester. I haven't seen the Knighthawks hockey team or the Rattlers play... whatever it is they play... oh, yes, lacrosse. I should brush up on lacrosse.

REFLECT, DISCUSS, BREATHE, CONNECT and THINK are just as necessary as "GO."

Anyway, I sometimes I have to remember that REFLECT, DISCUSS, BREATHE, CONNECT, and, most important, THINK, are verbs, too, and just as necessary to our family's well-being as "go."

So sometimes, WHOA is better than GO. If that's the case for you this week, then you heard it here first: Just. Don't. Do. It. That's right: DO NOT RUSH AROUND! Read a book with your kids, play a board game, paint your toenails, listen to some great music, wash your car, or... hey, how about wash *my* car?!

When Others Can Do It Better than We Can

I owe a lot to a lady who makes her living showing kids how to get around in tight, scary spaces.

Regina Race is the manager of Albany's Indoor Rock Gym, which has not only indoor rock climbing but the nation's only indoor spelunking. That's right: Built right into the walls of the building is a network of caves, with all manner of pitch-dark, mysterious tunnels leading to things like climbing nets, rooms full of mirrors, and even a zip line.

Most kids love the spelunking experience. But not my daughter Madison. She started to follow her friends into the tunnels, got to the first twist, and grimly backed out. "No way, no how," she said. Apparently, she has inherited a bit of my claustrophobia (I need to have free range of motion or I panic). It's difficult for me even to THINK about my child having the same experience. So even though in most circumstances, I would be the one cheerfully urging my kid to try this new thing, I just couldn't do it.

As much as we moms would love to think we can give our kids everything they need, so many people have so many other gifts that they are eager to share.

But Regina took the matter in hand. For almost 45 minutes, she talked Madison through the first part of the tunnel (about 15 feet). Not once did she lose patience. While Madison never really relaxed, neither did she panic. What Regina gave Madison was not comfort, exactly, but the know-how to have the courage it took to get up to the zip line. And afterward, she was very proud of herself for mastering her fear.

This is yet another reason why it's so important to get kids "out and about" in their communities: Much as we moms would love to think we can give our kids everything they need, so many people have so many other gifts that they are eager to share. I'm grateful to all of those like Regina, who give my kids what I can't.

The Season of NO

Is summertime the season of "No"?

Summer is second only to winter holidays in excuses for indulging ourselves a little. The pace of life slows. We are out of our usual routines. We go on vacation. We want our kids to see this time as special. It's a charmed time, when we'd love to say "yes" to as much as possible.

We take our kids on a special outing, and we want them to be happy, to mark it in their minds as a special day. So it's so tempting to say "Yes" to everything — to endless junk food, to colorful plastic souvenirs, to another ride on the whirly thing. But of course we can't do that, for the sake of everyone's health, our own wallets, and our sanity. We have to set limits, and because we can only say "Yes" a fraction of the time, it sometimes seems like summer is indeed the season of "No."

We take our kids on a special outing, and we want them to be happy, to mark it in their minds as a special day.

The best thing to do is to plan ahead when you're going somewhere, so that you know what will be offered and what to expect. (Hey, I can think of a cool web site for you to use!) Setting out in advance what you're willing to buy or do with your kids will cut down on (notice I didn't say eliminate) the on-site pleading, and will make you feel less like a big Scrooge when the time comes.

If your kids are older and you give them an allowance, you might even encourage them to save part of it specifically for vacation and special items they want to purchase, or activities they want to do. This has several benefits: It helps them learn the value of money, it teaches them about financial transactions, and it gives them decision-making power so that "no" becomes "that's not something our family will buy, but if you really want it, you have your allowance."

When the decision is in their hands, the whining disappears, you don't have to feel like Scrooge, and it's surprising how often they decide "no" for themselves...unless they really want it.

Five-Minute Glasses

When I was in my early 30s and learning how to organize my house, with two small children and a home-based business further complicating matters, I became a fan of the Fly Lady, Marla Cilley. Among lots of other tips for decluttering, organizing, and streamlining your life, she promotes a method called the 5-Minute Room Rescue.

It's easy to feel overwhelmed when your house (or life) is filled with clutter. We sense that it's going to take too long to fix, so we don't even try. But the Fly Lady points out that we usually CAN find 5 minutes.

Almost anything can be made better in 5 minutes. It's true.

I know that seems ridiculously short. But give it a try: Set the timer, focus, and GO. Do some dishes, wipe the counter, compost your wilted vegetables, pile the papers neatly. And STOP when the timer rings.

The Fly Lady's 5-Minute Rescue is not just good advice for home improvement; it works everywhere. Almost anything can be made better in 5 minutes. It's true. It works when your toddler is fussing in the grocery line, when your email box is overflowing, when you're frozen in traffic, when your spouse is fuming, when your daughter is distraught over flubbing the audition. Whatever.

First, put on your 5-Minute Glasses. Then, identify the problem (naming it is half the job). Next, take just 10 seconds to imagine a way you can improve the situation. Then do it for 5 minutes: Play "I Spy" with the toddler, do a manic little cleanup on the inbox, sing songs from *Frozen* while your car inches along, write a quick note to tell a distressed family member how much you love them. The world will be better than it was 5 minutes ago, and it will all be your fault. Feel good.

It's amazing what you can accomplish in 5 minutes. You can even write a perfectly adequate essay before the timer buz—

Consequences, Greek Style

Do you know the Greek myth about Icarus? He and his father, Daedalus, were imprisoned in a labyrinth on the island of Crete. To escape, Daedalus built wings made of feathers held together with wax. Despite warnings from his father, Icarus flew too close to the sun, which melted the wax, plummeting him into the sea.

The myth has been used as a cautionary tale for a couple thousand years to remind us not to get too big for our britches—to avoid reaching too high or else face punishment for our hubris. I even had an English teacher remind us that disobeying one's parents can sometimes carry a heavy penalty.

The idea that humans should stay complacently in our little places rather than strive for the highest heights is pernicious nonsense.

I always hated this story when I was a kid. I mean, DEATH as the punishment for ignoring your dad seemed unnecessarily harsh, to put it mildly. But my daughter is currently absorbed in Rick Riordan's *Percy Jackson* series, so lately I've had a fun opportunity to revisit some of those old Greek and Roman stories.

And yep, there it is. I still hate the Icarus and Daedalus myth. Because to me, the idea that humans should stay complacently in our little places rather than strive for the highest heights is pernicious nonsense. We're built to create, to achieve, to transcend... and to feel good about having done so.

I'd have been a lot happier with the story if Daedalus had instead encouraged Icarus to reach for the stars: "Don't let anyone hold you back, my son! You can do it...er, just maybe wait until after dark, okay? And whenever you fall, I'll be right underneath to catch you and help launch you back in the air."

My kids tell me that Daedalus isn't really any more impressive a parent in Rick Riordan's retelling of the story in *The Battle of the Labyrinth*. On the other hand, he does sort of redeem himself in the end, which apparently involves giving Annabeth his laptop. So that's a plus. I guess some myths are just hard to rewrite.

Failure as the Best Option

How often do you hear someone say, "FAILURE IS NOT AN OPTION!"?

In the movie *Apollo 13* (1995), Ed Harris, as Flight Director Gene Kranz, says it to his Houston team after an explosion depletes the oxygen supply on the Apollo 13 spacecraft. Mission Control's job is to get the men back down to solid ground without anyone exploding or asphyxiating. "Failure is not an option" works as a mantra to keep the team focused: Tom Hanks, Kevin Bacon, and Bill Paxton live to star in other movies, our American hearts swell with pride and relief, and we are all glad that no one gave up.

I believe we need to teach our kids to fail frequently, and fail responsibly. "Nothing ventured, nothing gained" is true.

But as a life strategy, or as a business strategy, or as a message you give to your kids, it's misguided. Sure, blowing off the important things in life, THAT'S not an option. But failure? Failure should be as familiar as the friend you call to come over for pizza and a *Big Bang Theory* marathon.

Deb, in this book, you keep telling us to embrace failure, practically to cuddle with it. What's up with that?

I know this book looks awfully normal from the outside, but it's true I keep pushing this radical idea of giving kids opportunities to fail—safely, of course. Can you tell I feel strongly about this?

What would happen if, this school year, you became less interested in your child's grades, and more interested in discovering and celebrating what your kids are learning for real—the actual math, reading, and logic skills, the history and science facts? It's harder, of course, to talk with kids about knowledge than to log in periodically and cast an eye over their latest quiz scores. But I think that overall you will find it lots more rewarding. And you'll probably even learn a lot!

I wish schools could mirror life more accurately. Of course, I understand that the massive system of education we have in our society, the sheer number of kids that must pass through the system—especially those whose parents don't care the way you do—means that we don't have the luxury of a custom education wherein each child can grow through their failures.

But if school has to be a place where you do everything you can to ensure success, well, what about failure? Think about using the upcoming school year to talk about the failure that inevitably comes when you push yourself to your limits. See if you can place greater stock in their failures than their A's. If they can get to that psychological place when they're young, they'll have years more in which to succeed.

Here's the secret truth about Apollo 13: Failure absolutely *was* an option. Did the Apollo 13 mission make it to the moon? No, the mission was aborted; the lunar landing was a total failure. Millions of dollars flushed into space. But is Apollo 13 a success story? You betcha.

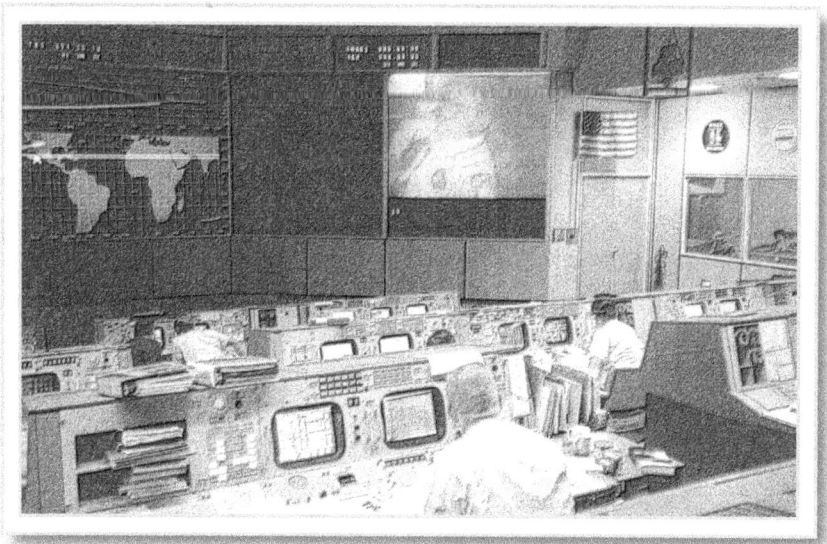

Photo: Public Domain Photo, courtesy of NASA

A Parent's Reflections on the Anniversary of 9/11

The five-year anniversary of the September 11 attacks was the first time my kids ever saw me cry.

On September 11, 2006, the girls and I were in a pizza restaurant in Virginia Beach. They were 5 and 7 years old. A television was playing high in a corner, and there was a replay of the second plane hitting the Twin Towers. "What's that?" Madison asked, and pointed, more in curiosity than horror. For all she knew, it was some kind of weird movie.

I had always been hesitant to cry in front of my kids, for several reasons: At a young age, kids can only handle so much, and a parent being out of control can be terribly frightening. I didn't want to worry them needlessly, either about me or what was on the screen. Plus, I had decided never to trivialize crying; in other words, I try to reserve it for times when it is particularly meaningful. (That is: Death merits tears. Burning the scrambled eggs, not so much.) In this case, of course, it was compounded by the fact that it is a mother's job to keep her kids safe... And on September 11, 2001, none of us felt safe.

But that day, September 11, 2006, I let the tears come. I was far from the only person in the place with dry eyes, though none of us was sobbing outright. I told my girls briefly what had happened five years earlier. It was the right moment to tell them, and the right way to tell them. They weren't scarred, but they understood something of the significance of the event. They have never forgotten that day.

Every family handles these issues differently. I was fortunate that my kids were babies when the attacks happened, and I could choose how and when to tell them about that awful day. Others did not have it easy; kids expect—and deserve—to be brought up in safety and love. For some older kids, even outside of the regions where the attacks occurred, their world was rocked as much as ours was.

These many years later, I find it easier to talk about the events with my kids, in large part because our country hasn't suffered anything close to that scale since. (Knock wood and all that.) I can't look at a military serviceperson without feeling awash in gratitude. (To all who serve or have loved ones in the armed forces: Thank you.)

Those of you who were readers back in 2001 remember what KidsOutAndAbout.com readers did as a small gesture of solidarity:

You created online messages for the front line responders in the NYC emergency services and sent them to us. We printed hundreds and gave them to my neighbor, who was an EMT. She brought them in her truck to New York to help encourage these brave people. It helped us remember the value of communities spontaneously working together to alleviate suffering.

I invite you, each September 11, to spend a few minutes with the memories of this day, either alone or with your kids. A few minutes to remember what is right, what is important, what is good... and to think about what we can do to preserve our future for our children.

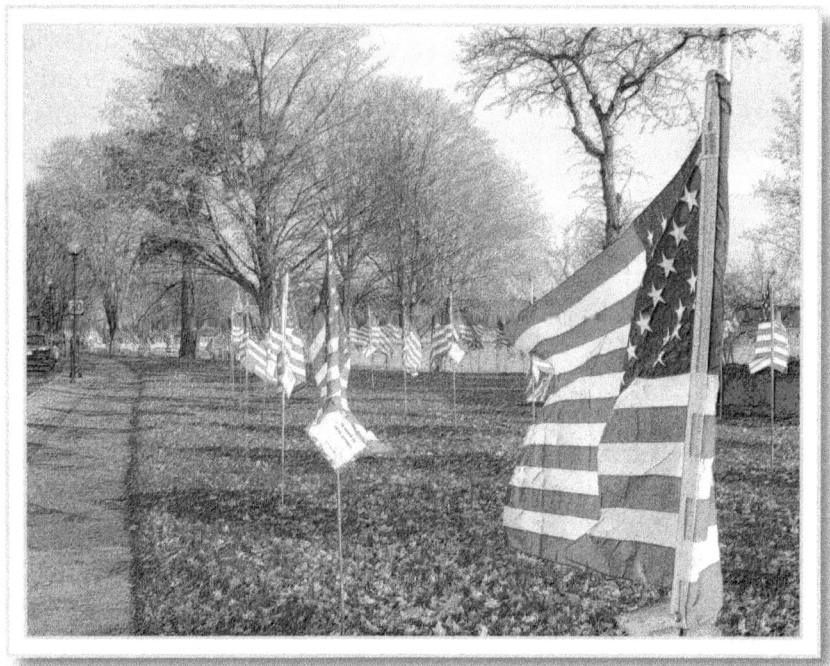

Gloom and Doom and...School

This is the time of year when I realize afresh how so many of my parenting decisions and even seasonal moods are influenced by what happened during my childhood. When I was a kid, despite doing well in school, I loathed it. To me, it felt like a prison from which I couldn't escape until I was an adult. So every summer, Labor Day loomed like Doomsday. Nowadays, despite my not having been in school for over 20 years—and, even more ridiculous, despite the fact that my own kids are home schooled—late August still brings me that sense of must-cram-in-fun-before-it-all-ends-in-misery desperation that I experienced from about third grade onward.

Late August still brings me that sense of must-cram-in-fun-before-it-all-ends-in-misery....

I have to work hard this time of year to be upbeat, so that my family only experiences the benefit of some extra fun without the gloom. Kinda silly, no? But there it is.

What can you do to help offset this? How about some of the following ideas:

Look at your summer wish list of things you wanted to do this summer, or discover what your kids would still like to fit in, and get busy doing!

Make a list of things you want to do during the fall and winter, once school starts, and put them on the schedule so you have activities and adventures to look forward to (KidsOutAndAbout.com can help with the planning)!

Set up a weekly game or activity "date night" with the whole family to add sparkle to your week!

Once school starts, have the kids keep a list on the refrigerator, or a journal of all the GOOD things that happened each day. Preserve the lists from week to week and year to year, as a reminder that life doesn't end with the start of school.

Where's Papa Going with That Axe?

"Where's Papa going with that axe?"
The opening line of Charlotte's Web is one of the most compelling in all of children's literature. Where IS Papa going with that axe? That one sentence launches us brilliantly into the next 192 pages, and part of E.B. White's genius is that everything that happens is shaped by those six little words.

Starting off on the right foot matters. But I think endings matter even more. Our lives are composed of story arcs small and large, and how we bring one to conclusion means everything to how we incorporate its meaning into our lives. End a chapter with class, with a little a ta-da!, and the story will cast a rosy glow over the rest of life. End it with a fizzle and it will fade into irrelevance and be forgotten. End it with bitterness and the whole story will be colored black, and the regret will linger forever.

Bring your summmer to a close with class.... You could end it with a bang, like a trip to an amusement park, or with a series of gentle whispers, like with s'mores around a campfire or a day flying kites.

Fortunately, we can often choose our own endings to chapters, even those that are mostly out of our control. Consider two people losing their jobs through downsizing: One throws a party for the colleagues who have meant the most to him during his time there, the other tosses the contents of his desk into a box and storms out. Not only does the first guy get to look back on that period of his life and see a rainbow instead of a thundercloud, but that party could be exactly what launches him into the next chapter of his career.

It's the same with the end of summer, which can be especially wrenching for kids: To them, it often means giving up something that they love for something they like...um... not so much. So here is my advice: Bring summer to a close with class: Get out and about! You could end it with a bang, like with a trip to an amusement park, or with a series of gentle whispers, like with s'mores around a campfire or a day flying kites. Your finale should be in your family's own style, but something memorable, something that casts a golden hue back on this summer. And let your closing line also be the creative beginning that launches you into the next chapter. This fall could be a bestseller! So start it compellingly.

Probably best to leave the axe at home, though.

P.S. Maybe you were wondering how Charlotte's Web ends. Here it is: "It is not often that someone comes along who is a true friend and a good writer. Charlotte was both."

Good to the last drop, that E.B. White.

Fall

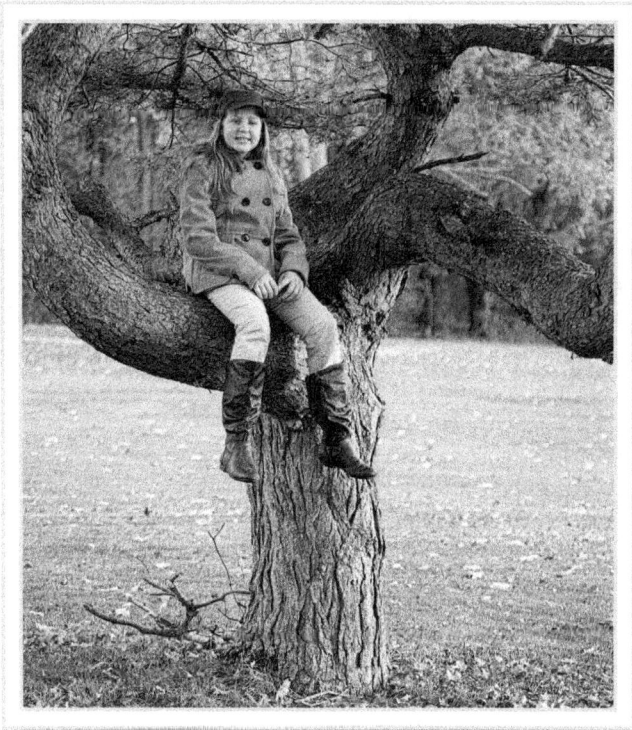

Photo: Honey DeLapa

Inch by Inch, Everything's a...

One gorgeous October day when I was in my early twenties, my group of friends decided to go hiking for a day in the Catskills. It was a very tall mountain, or at least so it seemed to me. I was among the stragglers huffing and puffing as we brought up the rear.

Our leader called down to us, "Come on, people! Inch by inch, everything's a cinch!"

"Maybe, Bill, but we're going yard by yard. That's a different rhyme!" I shouted back, ever the smart aleck.

Going inch by inch is sometimes the only way to succeed.

Here's the thing: Bill and I were both right, and it's worth remembering this as we kick off the school year.

Going inch by inch is sometimes the only way to succeed. Try to game the system with a helicopter ride to the top, and you'll end up alienating people and sliding down your own personal hill. For instance, KidsOutAnd-About had two million readers in 2014. But that took 13-and-a-half years to accomplish. There aren't any shortcuts to bringing happy readers back to a web site for repeat visits: We've progressed inch by inch, article by article, newsletter by newsletter, organization by organization, reader by reader.

But going yard by yard has its points, too. To grow as people or as a business, we need constantly to be pushing ourselves, extending ourselves, testing ourselves to see how much we can accomplish. Break your goals down into inch-by-inch increments so you can see what needs to be done. And then: Full steam ahead! No question about it: You'll change direction often and fail frequently. But if you celebrate every inch, every yard, every mile, the unrelenting pursuit of excellence is rewarding all through the journey, not just at the end.

Stop and Smell the Basil

If the school year would follow Deb's calendar, it would start in October.

Have you noticed how both our body rhythms and family rhythms follow the weather and seasons? In winter, we inhale the brisk air on sunny days and cozy up when Mother Nature encourages hibernation. When life returns in spring, we want to get out in that newly-warm sun, start all kinds of things growing, and launch all kinds of plans. In the summer, we move slower, and even though we're cultivating what we've planted, we want to do it at a relaxed pace. When the heat loses a bit of its grip in September, we become saturated with abundance: fruit and veggies are plentiful and less expensive, tomatoes are fire-red with pink insides instead of anemic orange, and everyone is giving you all their spare eggplant and cabbage.

> *Too seldom do we stop and pat ourselves on the back for an achievement; instead, we zoom off to the next item on our to-do list*

I was in the pick-your-own plot of my local farm this week in the green bean row—it comes with being a member of the CSA—and I still almost couldn't believe my luck. All I can pick? Seriously? This is amazing.

So September is the payoff part of summer, the celebration time, the dude-we-grew-that-and-yes-it-will-feed-a-nation-for-another-year time. But our society artificially pushes us into fall. We sense somehow that we should be celebrating... but instead, we rev up with school and new routines. This is par for the course in our hectic society: Too seldom do we stop and pat ourselves on the back for an achievement; instead, we zoom off to the next item on our to-do list

But I feel strongly that we should stop and smell the basil. Fortunately, this is the time not only of the harvest, but of the harvest festival! Fall festivals provide the perfect excuse for your family to celebrate abundance and the fact that we as humans can enjoy it. So hit the snooze button on your fall alarm clock. Stop and smell the basil.

There's Treasure Everywhere

One of my favorite books is a Calvin & Hobbes compilation called *There's Treasure Everywhere*. Like many of Bill Watterson's Calvin & Hobbes cartoons, the cover graphic reminds us that so much of what adults see as ordinary, boring, or even kind of disgusting are exciting new discoveries to a kid. Snow brings joy. Filling up the bathroom sink with minty green toothpaste designs brings joy. Worms bring joy. The fact that you can fog up the car window and draw a smiley face brings joy. That cloud that looks like a bunny, it brings joy too, all the more profound for keeping its shape only a minute.

Kids are the ultimate treasure hunters. They are made richest by the treasures they discover all on their own.

When my daughter Madison was a toddler, her first-time delight in something new was often accompanied by what we called The Face: a look of almost-trembling, wide-eyed astonishment at the new wonder in her world. David and I lived for The Face. We raced to show her things, to help her touch and taste and hear and smell, to give her opportunities to demonstrate that she could make things happen in her world, just to see that look, that beautiful oh-my-gosh-I've-discovered-something-AMAZING look.

Kids are the ultimate treasure hunters. Just think of their favorite indoor game: Hide and seek. There's nothing like that little jolt of joy when you discover your sister crammed into the laundry hamper, even if she hides there every time she's not It. And what kid doesn't love digging randomly in the dirt, just like Calvin? You never know what you'll find under there, or what your imagination will do with what you'll find.

I use the tour-guide-to-the-world metaphor to describe the special role parents have in introducing their kids to new experiences. The best part comes, though, when the kid becomes the tour guide to the treasures he has just discovered.

One place you'll find neverending treasure: Your local library! My recommendation for when you go: Bring your kids to the children's section, nudge them gently in the direction of books that might inter-est them or introduce them to the children's librarian, and then back off for a bit and see what happens. Kids are made richest by the treasures they discover all on their own.

Worried? Just Sprinkle on Some Math

I recently ordered a birthday present for my daughter from a master artisan in Indiana. His web site was not very sophisticated; it didn't even have an ordering mechanism. I located his email address in the small print, and emailed him to ask how to place an order. He emailed me back, telling me the price. "I'm going to the post office tomorrow," he added. "If you want one, just tell me you'll put the check in the mail, email me your address, and I'll send it to you."

"You'll send it to me before I've paid you?" I asked, astonished. What I was ordering wasn't worth a fortune, but it was no $5 item, either.

He told me that when you do the math, you realize that the risk of a problem is actually very small. "I prefer to live this way," he said. "Less anxiety."

When you do the math, you feel better. Hmm.

Of course, this made me think about parenting. (That's my job, after all.) So I thought about how doing math to calculate risk might apply to parenting.

Today's parents tend to be hyper-cautious about what we let our kids try, much more so than our own parents were. In today's multimedia world, if something bad happens to a child somewhere, that fact is instantly recorded and hyped into millions of homes, retweeted from millions of Twitter accounts, shoved into millions of faces... graphically. Fear sells. If a child gets injured, everyone looks first at the blood and then at the lawyers. So we compete to rubber-room our kids' environments, because we have the sense that the greater the lengths we go to keep our kids safe, the better parents we are. We must protect them from everything bad, right? But the actual data on crime in the U.S. tells a different story than the media does: It shows that our world is actually safer than it was when we were kids. What does this mean?

It means that when one of my kids wants to do something that could be dangerous (walk to the store, climb a tree, navigate the hiking trail solo, play in the creek, bike to the library...things most of us did on our own when we were kids), I try to ask myself: What are the actual chances that something horrible will happen? Is the reward (my child's independence and confidence in her ability to navigate the world) worth the risk? I try to do an actual cost-benefit analysis instead of allowing my emotions free play, focusing on the facts that will let me calculate the real probability of a problem. I ask myself: "What are the chances that she might actually die or be scarred for life?" If I determine that the risk of death or serious injury, given her ability, is smaller than riding in a car, I take a deep breath, push away the images that the CNN of my imagination is trying to play in my brain, and let her do it.

Do the math. Be sensible. Don't worry. Be happy.

Be the Karma, Part 2

I was thinking this week about the difference between success and excellence.

KidsOutAndAbout's mission is to celebrate excellence. Editors in each of our regions make a point of finding and promoting the organizations that provide the resources that give your kids opportunities to learn, grow, become culturally literate, and have fun. By celebrating these organizations and the people behind them, we help get the word out so that they can...

SUCCEED.

And by succeed, I mean survive and thrive so they can keep right on being excellent. See, this is KidsOutAndAbout's real mission. Sure, I love it that some of those organizations find it worthwhile to pay us for extra visibility in the form of advertising; it lets us run the site, earn a living, spread to new regions. But really, this whole cheerleader gig I've got going is mostly for the purpose of changing the world. I want more of the good stuff to be out there so that more of you get to experience it, now and in the future. In 30 years, I want my future grandchildren to experience the local activities my daughters grew up with, such as jazz at the Harley School's Bebop to Bach concerts and Renaissance paintings at the Memorial Art Gallery; I want them to take tuba lessons at Hochstein School of Music & Dance and go on nature hikes at Letchworth State Park, and pick apples at Brown's Berry Patch and watch star shows in Strasenburgh Planetarium. Similarly-excellent resources appear throughout our country, in your own back yard, wherever creative people are given free rein.

Excellence is different from success. Your own excellence is pretty much under your control: Work like heck for years, with focus and passion and dedication, and you'll be excellent. The people who provide resources for kids in our community understand this concept. Check. Done. But...will these places succeed? Will they survive into the future? That depends on whether our community turns out to support them now. And it also depends on things we can't control, like the economy and the weather.

Think about all of the fall festivals and harvest farms and apple orchards and pumpkin patches that rely on weekend weather in October. The folks who run these places provide a great deal of value to our community and wonderful experiences for our kids; after so many years running this site, I have gotten to know most of them personally. This year, October's weekend weather has been pretty much insert-bad-word-here. Add that to the April freeze that devastated much of the apple crop and you've got a recipe for hardship. So, my dear KidsOutAndAbout readers: If you've been waiting for the ideal weekend to help your kids make autumn memories and experience the best of what fall has to offer in our region, use this one. If Mother Nature is unkind on Saturday and Sunday, please take a page from what the Scandinavians say: There is no such thing as bad weather, only the wrong clothes.

And if you know of some organizations doing excellent things that could use a little public praise, BE THE KARMA. Tell your friends, post to your favorite social network, send a letter to the editor. It matters.

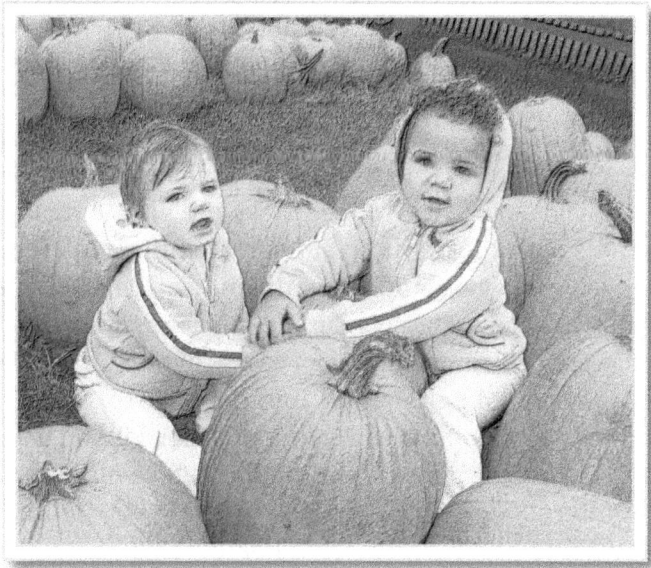

Photo: Dresden Engle

Thank the Real People

When I was a kid, whenever we received excellent service at a restaurant, my mother always made a point of finding the manager as we were on our way out; she would name the waiter or waitress and say exactly what she appreciated. She explained to me that this was a way both of saying "thank you" and of reinforcing what was good.

I've tried to carry through this principle with my own kids, not just in restaurants, but with anyone who provides something of value to our family or community. I guess I've taken it one step further—because the whole mission of KidsOutAndAbout is to celebrate, publicly, the resources in our area that help enrich our kids and families. It's my way of both saying "thank you" and of trying to help preserve these organizations for the next generation.

Showing your appreciation takes only a few clicks and a few minutes...but it means a lot.

In the past few years, social media has made it all the more easy for us regular people to give feedback, and also to make personal connections with those who create great stuff. I was reminded of this fact when my girls and I saw the movie *Atlas Shrugged Part 2*. I thought the best character in the movie was portrayed by Esai Morales, whom you may remember as one of the stars of NYPD Blue in its later years. My girls and I found his portrayal of Francisco D'Anconia so compelling that the next morning I found his Facebook page and sent a short note of appreciation. It took me only 2 minutes. But that afternoon, he sent me back a lovely note telling me how much it meant to him to hear what I had to say.

So think about this the next time you and your kids read a terrific book, see a play, visit an exhibit, hear a concert, or take part in a community festival. Help your family remember that real people made it happen, and that showing your appreciation takes only a few clicks and a few minutes... but it means a lot.

Dry Blankets Are Cozier Than Wet Ones

For many years, I've spent my Friday mornings on the radio. Last week, the regular show hosts and I were discussing our favorite seasons, because it had just turned to autumn officially. I was saying how my kids and husband love the fall, but that I personally prefer early summer. The hosts, Tony Infantino and Kristie Credit, were exactly in tune with me, and for the same reasons: "Fall would be great," we all agreed, "If only it didn't lead to... WINTER."

We were having this discussion off the air, because it's important when you're doing a family-oriented radio show to focus on the POSITIVE. No one likes a wet blanket. Fortunately, this is not hard to do, because there are lots of sides to every situation, and all kinds of ways to find and focus on good things. And Tony and Kristie are fabulous at turning anything into a joke. So we can talk about all of the totally true reasons to love fall: the crispness in the air that makes everyone more energetic and productive, the wonderful tastes of the harvest, all of the fall festivals and activities that are available because everyone knows that winter is JUST AROUND THE CORNER and we're all trying to cram in stuff before the snow flies. Oops, sorry, wait, can't go there. Must stay positive! This is family-oriented!

Have you noticed that parenting is like that, too? Even if you feel at the end of your rope when your 3-year-old says "You can't make me!" for the hundredth time that day, you calmly and creatively find ways to give him choices. Even if you think your child's violin sounds like the banshees on their way to Hades (I know, I'm mixing cultural traditions there), you say things like, "I just love how hard you've been working on that piece. Play some more." And even if you're feeling doubts that you're up to the New-New Math that your 6th grader has brought home for homework, you smile and give it your best shot. That is: As a parent, even if what you feel inside is something different than what you're choosing to express, what you show can still be totally true and authentic. It's just careful.

I think that's probably the mark of a good leader: To be able to clearly see all sides of an issue, and then nurture the positive while diminishing the effect of the negative. I try my best to be this way, too. Remember this during the second week of February when it's insanely cold and snowy out there and it seems winter will never

END, and I'm cheerfully telling you about the best places to go ice skating...you can be pretty sure that at the same time, inside I'm shivering right along with you.

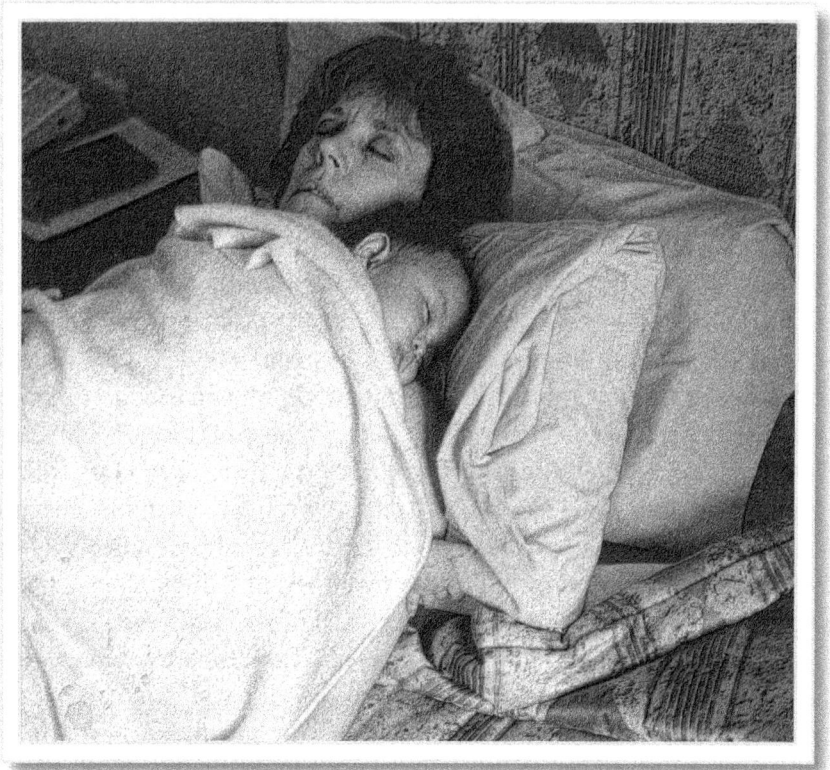

Photo: Ted Llewellyn

Taking the Fish to Church

As part of the Excelsior Fife & Drum Corps—Madison plays fife and Ella plays drum—my kids often are called upon to play at ceremonies and memorials as well as parades and living history events. Recently, they were playing at a ceremony that included a Mass at which the Corps all sat in the front. "When in Rome, do as the Romans do" can be very useful when you find yourself in a situation where you don't quite know what you're doing, and on Sunday that literally proved to be the case. Ella, age 11, is able pretty easily to go with the flow, but Madison, 13, analyzes everything, and worries about whether anyone else can tell she doesn't really know what she's doing.

"I know you were uncomfortable sitting in the front of the church in your uniform," I told her afterward. "But no one could tell. I know you're often in that kind of situation, where you don't feel you can relax because you're not completely familiar with the routine, but you're doing great, and it builds character."

Feeling like a fish out of water is part of what late childhood and early teenagerhood is all about.

"Mom, I'm *always* uncomfortable," she said. "All the time, everywhere. It's just the way you are when you're 13."

Of course, she was right. Feeling like a fish out of water is part of what late childhood and early-teenagerhood is all about: You're growing so fast, and the expectations are changing on you so quickly, that it's hard to relax and be yourself—whoever that is that week— especially around your peers who are in the same position. I think this is partly why family traditions are so important: They are the reliable life experiences that help to keep our kids steady while everything else whips by them dizzyingly fast.

And there are so many comforting traditions available in fall, traditions that remain the same no matter how quickly the world changes. These are sensory experiences, too—corn mazes and apple picking and pumpkins and hot apple cider—and they imprint themselves on our kids' memories for a lifetime. If your kids are young,

I'd suggest establishing your fall family traditions now so that they can rely on them year after year. And if your kids are older, make sure that the whole family participates in these traditions so that your kids have something solid to think about fondly in the midst of a busy teenage life. It only takes two consecutive years of doing something memorable to make a tradition, so go for it!

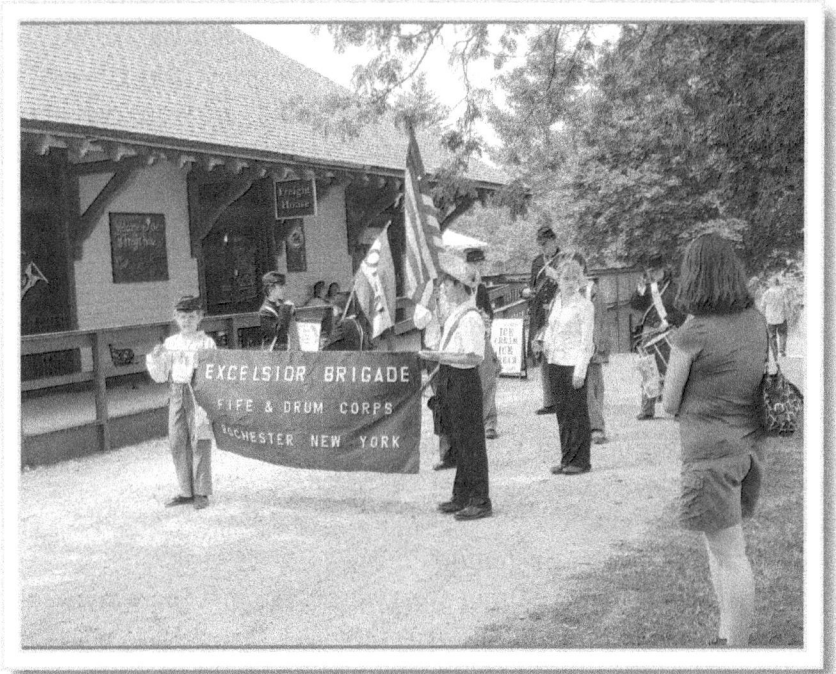

Practice Leads to Better Things Than Broadway

Working toward goals and accomplishing them seems to me to be a critical component of a happy life, whether you're a kid or an adult. Some people are naturally goal-oriented from a very early age, and something inside them drives them to work hard. Others are not as naturally driven and need some external coaching and encouragement to help them realize what they want to do and be motivated to persist until the accomplishment is theirs.

Parents who have more than one child know that they can have very different personalities from one another. This is the case in my family, especially on this dimension. Because Madison (at least at this stage) seems

It's the parent's job to start cheering right fron the beginning.

more internally driven than Ella, I have to remind myself that this doesn't mean that Ella needs achievement any less; rather, she needs me to cheer her on a bit more to boost her out of her comfort zone and encourage her to persist at things so that she can take pride in accomplishments that are all her own.

I've tried to help the girls identify small goals so we can get them used to the happy zing of achievement. Learning to play a musical instrument is one of those journeys that can be either gratifying in the short-term or not, depending on how the parent treats it. Kids aren't great at long journeys on their own. Practicing can get discouraging for the child, because the payoff can seem so far away. But one of the good things about practicing, whether it's a musical instrument or another skill like handwriting or sports or exercise, is that you can only get better at it, and you can measure your progress. I believe it's the parent's job to start cheering right from the beginning. And when they hit milestones, name them, write them down, and cheer even louder.

Here. You can borrow my megaphone.

Pushing Your Worry Button

This was my lunchtime conversation yesterday. I bet you've been there, in some form:

Me: "For pity's sake, Madison…Learn to use the napkin!"

Madison: "You know, I won't have this problem with MY daughter."

Me: "No? Why not?"

Madison: "*I* will not have been a failure as a mother."

It is sometimes very hard to remember that regardless of how hard a parent might push on something, the child has her own natural pace….

She was kidding (I think!), but she knew she was tapping on that little worry button all mothers have. The fun never ends when you're a parent, does it? Or the effort. Or the need for patience. I'm sorry to tell those of you with younger kids who are wondering whether by age 12 they'll remember to place their napkin on their laps that the answer is: Maybe some of the time. It is sometimes very hard to remember that regardless of how hard a parent might push on something, a child has her own natural developmental pace, that may or may not fit with our (or society's) expectations.

The flip side of the frustration that we might feel is that this also presents endless opportunities for small celebrations. For example, my younger daughter was very slow to warm up to reading. "Someday she'll understand that it's fun, someday she really will…" I chanted to myself for years. Before she turned 12, there were no magical "ah-ha" moments for Ella as there are for some kids; progress was slow but fairly steady.

On the other hand, this means that I got to notice and privately rejoice at every small milestone, such as the one when she decided to take *Little Town on the Prairie* into the car to read because she wanted to find out what happened. A first! (Bless you, Laura Ingalls Wilder.)

It All Makes Me Want to Jump Up and Down

The other evening, my kids and I were in the grocery store parking lot when an enthusiastic young lady from the local TV station approached us, cameraman in tow.

"We're interviewing parents for an upcoming story," she said. "Would you be willing to give us an opinion on camera?"

"Sure," I said, never one to shun the limelight. We positioned Ella next to me. The lights blazed.

"We're talking about bounce houses tonight!" the reporter said. "There has been some word of danger with kids in bounce houses." She looked at me expectantly.

"Oh," I said. I must have looked pretty blank. I certainly felt blank.

"Would you let your kids jump in a bounce house?" she asked.

"Well, sure," I said. "I'd have to have some actual evidence about something being dangerous before I'd ban them from doing what they've done a hundred times before without a problem. If it's just something like how they're more likely to knock heads while they're bouncing, well, they do that often enough at home anyway."

I'm pretty sure I didn't make the 11 o'clock news that night; it seemed that what the reporter was looking for was the opposite of what I gave her. Calm common sense—the desire to have more information before forming an opinion—doesn't make for good TV. Should the mere suggestion that something might be dangerous send us mothers into protective hysteria to save our kids from the looming what-ifs? I don't think so.

I actually feel pretty passionately about this. Not about bounce houses, of course; aside from having watched my kids jump in them for years, I have no basis for forming an opinion about their supposed dangers. But the idea that my uninformed knee-jerk opinion is valuable for TV viewers: That's where I have the problem. Who cares what I think about the engineering of today's bounce houses? I'm a publisher, not a physicist or a physician.

It all makes me want to ... jump up and down.

Fear Works

Consider two articles that might be published on KidsOutAndAbout's site:

10 Shocking Activities Your Kids Will Miss If They Stay Inside: Ignore These at Your Peril!

10 Great Ways for Kids and Families to Enjoy Autumn Outside

Actually, these both would link to the same article; they just have different titles. Have you noticed that more and more, articles on the internet have titles similar to the first one, even on reputable sites? These publishers live and die by the numbers. They want to compel you to click, so they do it by arousing your fear rather than your calm, well-reasoned interest. Sadly, it works, especially for good parents. I guarantee that if I were to publish both of these and then I looked at the statistics, the first link would have more clicks.

It is sometimes very hard to remember that regardless of how hard a parent might push on something, the child has her own natural pace....

Fear works, but is it a good idea? I say NO. We don't play on your fear at KidsOutAndAbout. Our mission is to be happy but realistic cheerleaders. We investigate, we gather, we guide, we point, we celebrate, but we don't hype. When you access our articles and lists, we want you to feel smart, not duped.

Fear "works" in parenting, too, at least in the short term. Sure, you can make your kids shut up and do what you say quickly by arousing their anxiety over possible consequences. But does it ultimately have the effect you want? That's up to you to decide, of course. I find that as I get older, being motivated to move toward something positive pushes me toward my goals much faster—and makes my day-to-day existence much happier—than fear of something bad happening. So that's how I'm trying to inspire my kids to learn to work, to focus, to do the right thing: By painting a picture of the pot of gold at the end of the rainbow and relentlessly waving my pom-poms in that direction.

I hope what you read in this book has inspired you. If it makes you afraid, let me know, and I'll fire the writer.

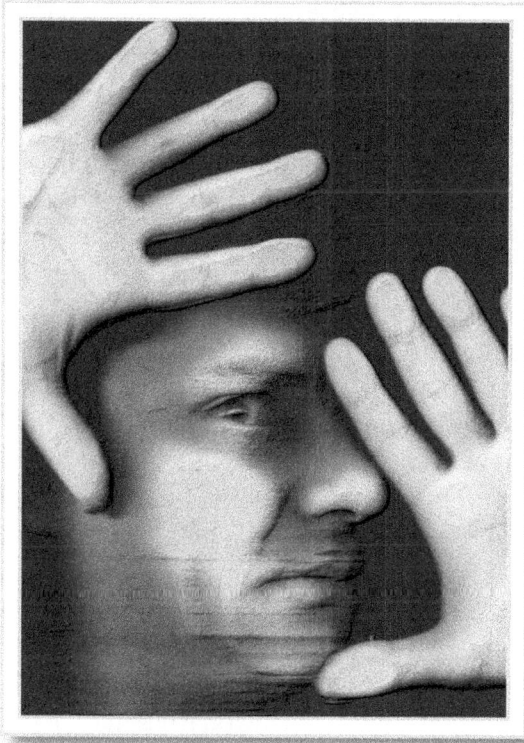

Photo: Santiago Cornejo

Masks

October is a great time to think about masks, and role-playing.

Kids are in a constant process of discovering who they are, and who they are going to be. I maintain, though, that it's less a process of self-discovery than self-creation. Becoming who you are going to become is a decision—actually, a million decisions made at a million tiny forks in the road. Your comfort in this life-long process rests fundamentally in your attitude about it: Are we humans simply at the mercy of our own genetic code and our environment, like a dandelion spore blowing in the wind, with little control over the end result? Or are we more like pilots at the helm of a ship, with how we navigate the choppy waters of life making all the difference?

One of the single most helpful things we can do as parents is to help kids understand that how they think, how they act, and how they respond becomes increasingly under their control as they grow. To that end, role-playing is a great tool for kids, even if it is sometimes inconvenient for parents. By role-playing, I mean those phases that kids go through where they're trying on an attitude, a way of doing things, a way of talking. Like the Teenage Mutant Ninja Turtles Phase, the Hannah Montana Phase, the High School Musical Phase. I remember my Wonder Woman phase from the late '70s; I'm sure that wasn't very convenient for my parents, but boy did I feel powerful.

And that's what it's all about: Trying on roles like we try on masks at Halloween, figuring out what fits and why. So be patient, friends... the "role" phase only lasts... well, all of childhood, and beyond.

Photo: Debra E. Ross

A Watched Maple Tree Never Explodes

A watched maple tree never bursts into color.

When I was growing up in Cranford, NJ, I was a big leaf-pile jumper. I didn't consider fall really to have arrived until the silver maple in my front yard turned yellow and dropped its leaves into rake-able piles. The only problem was that mine was always the last tree in the neighborhood to turn, and so it would be a full month between when the calendar said it was fall and when my personal fall actually arrived. A month is forever as far as a 6-year-old is concerned.

Nowadays, if I'm not careful, I will blink, and it will be Thanksgiving.

How can we grownups simultaneously slow down time for ourselves and make the season vivid for our kids? The answer is simple, really: PLAN! Don't just let the fall happen, or it will be over before you've done anything. Planning gives you something to look forward to, which both helps slow down time for adults and builds up anticipation for kids.

How can we grownups simultaneously slow down time for ourselves and make the season memorable for our kids? The answer is simple, really: PLAN!

So when you're looking at your local online community calendar, don't just check out this weekend's events, look at the next weekend's, and the next! Plan to do some traditional fall activities, like a corn maze, pumpkin patch, apple picking, or fun on the farm, and talk it up in advance! At the very least, talk about what you're going to do when the leaves finally fall and the whole family gets to rake.

Of course if you're lucky enough to have a maple tree handy, watch it! Time will slow down. Trust me.

Honeycrisps Always Ripen First

You can't make a Granny Smith ripen before a Honeycrisp.

So said a wise farmer. You can plant a Granny Smith apple tree right next to a Honeycrisp apple tree. You can nurture them similarly, keep them fertilized and watered and pruned alike and shoo the pests away from both. But nothing you can do will make that Granny Smith apple ripen at the same time as a Honeycrisp apple. Each has its own distinct nature, its own schedule, its own rhythm.

So it goes with children. If you have more than one, as I do, then you know that Child #2 is as full of surprises as Child #1 was. We forget about the fact that one is a Granny Smith and one is a Honeycrisp, so we're surprised when they mature at different paces. We expect that as long as we treat them the same, and nurture them well, and if they're both working hard at learning and growing, then we can expect essentially the same results. They'll take their first steps, learn to read, develop empathy, attack Algebra, decide to date, and learn to drive a car at exactly the time when society expects them to, if we've done our jobs right as parents. Right?

Ha.

Look around at your Facebook friends from high school: As a rule, are today's happiest, healthiest, most engaged and productive adults the same people who were the stars from way back when? Probably not. The Granny Smiths who found what they love to do and work hard at it are doing just as well as the Honeycrisps. Fancy that.

Thanksgiving for Modern Medicine

Last Tuesday, I got a call from our VP of Operations, June Santini. I was not expecting anything startling, because June and I are on the phone with each other constantly. But before I even said hello, she shouted "Oh my GOSH!" right into my ear.

Now, June does not typically shout, except maybe at a wayward teenager, and then only if it's one of hers. So I thought for sure something was wrong. "What? WHAT?" I asked, a little panicky.

"Our web site is GORGEOUS!" she said, without lowering even a decibel.

"You mean the new master guide to the holidays page?" I asked. I had just put it together, and while I think it's wonderfully useful, it didn't seem that it deserved actual yells of delight.

"You don't GET it!" she said. "I can SEE it now! The whole site. The colors are amazing!"

See, last week June had cataract surgery, which—I learned from her—is the most common operation in the United States. They replace the entire lens of your eye with an artificial one, which not only removes the cataract (put simply, a clouding) but which, if you have poor vision generally, makes you able to see better than you ever have before. June had the surgery in one eye on Monday; by Tuesday, the bandage was off, and her vision in that eye was perfect. Yesterday, she had the surgery in the other eye, and the bandage comes off this morning. (I'll be careful to hold the receiver away from my ear when I answer the phone today.)

So as you can imagine, June is feeling thankful for modern medicine these days. I am, too, on her behalf. The timing is perfect, don't you think? Many of us are in the mode of counting our blessings this week, and I'm thinking about all of the people I love who are still walking on the planet thanks to modern medicine. And now, so are you!

Consider the Source

Growing up, I spent a lot of time at my friend Anne's house. Anne's mom was smart and liked to talk, and she said lots of things that were worth listening to. Here was my favorite: When Anne and I would complain about a snooty or hurtful comment that some other kid had flung our way, Mrs. Haughney had a great phrase: Consider the source.

Consider the source. Three little words, the meaning of which really were: "I'm so sorry you felt hurt, but this person does not make it her practice to add value to the world, does she? Instead, she tries to tear other people down. She hasn't grown up yet. Such people are not worthy of being taken seriously. You are, though. So try not to worry about it."

It helped. It helped a lot.

As I grew up, I discovered that, unfortunately, even some adults prefer to tear people down rather than build something wonderful. So I coined a phrase I have found helpful, one that binds in the implicit gratitude that follows from "consider the source": He HAS to be him, you GET to be you. In other words, feel grateful that you chose to become someone who builds rather than destroys, and feel pity for those who chose that unhappy path. Try not to let them get under your skin.

> *He HAS to be him, you GET to be you. It's a magical phrase. And it works best when we tell it to good people who need encouragement.*

He HAS to be him, you GET to be you. It's a magical phrase. And it works best when we tell it to good people who need encouragement. So say it to your adult friends having trouble at work, say it to your kids as they struggle to deal with others growing up in this big messy world, and say it to yourself when unruly relatives threaten the peace of your holiday gathering. And at Thanksgiving, consider including a silent word of thanks to the people in your life who make every interaction a blessing. They matter.

Chinese Food and the Norm Effect

I frequent my favorite Chinese restaurant for two reasons: Good food, and the Norm Effect.

Those of you of a certain age remember the TV show *Cheers*. "Cheers" was the name of a bar in Boston "where everybody knows your name." That was most true of Norm Peterson: Whenever he'd walk into Cheers, everyone in the bar would shout, "NORM!" That warm sense of welcoming recognition is now known in our culture as the Norm Effect.

I feel like Norm whenever I walk into Vicky Shi's restaurant, Hong Wah. Vicky knows the names of hundreds of her regular customers. When she spots me, she enthusiastically calls out, "Hi, Deb!" She knows what I am about to order (broccoli with garlic sauce). She asks after the kids.

That warm sense of welcoming recognition from the TV show Cheers "where everybody knows your name" is now known in our culture as the Norm Effect.

Vicky makes each and every customer feel not only welcome, but visible. Somehow, she conveys that she's happy you're there, and that you're you, and that you should be happy, too. And the food is great.

Over a decade ago, Harvard professor Robert Putnam discussed his idea of "social capital" in a book called *Bowling Alone*. He talks about the importance of being connected with others in social networks. He claims that "joining and participating in one group" (presumably in person...not a Facebook group) "cuts in half your risk of dying next year." It has something to do with the sense of validation and purpose one gets from being connected in the world. I don't know about that, though it does make me wonder: If each of us had a Vicky, would we all live longer? Even if not, doesn't it mean we all live better?

But you can't go ordering up Vickies like you can Chinese food, right? Wait, maybe you can! We have kids, don't we? My theme is often some variant of "Be the Karma." How about we all teach our kids to Be the Vicky for the people we encounter every day out in the world? If we all just do this, it might even become... dare I say it... the Norm.

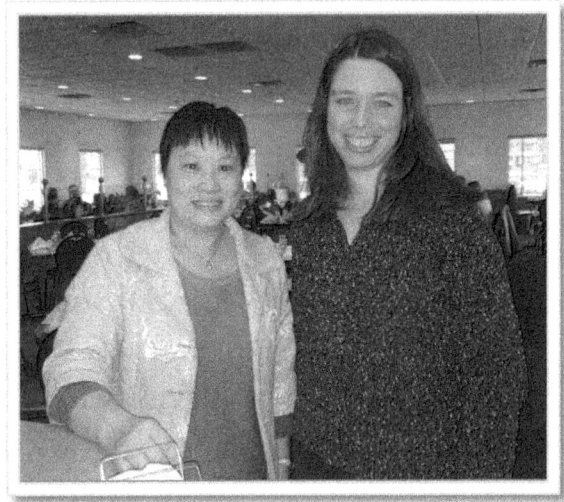

Photo: Ella Ross

Thinking in Stories

It's the time of the year for... stories. There's nothing like a chill in the air and the holidays underfoot to make us want to snuggle down on a couch for a cup of tea and conversation.

Some stories are family legends, like the time Grandpa caught a hero fly ball barehanded during a stickball street championship game but never had his pinkie reset properly so that's why it looks like that. Some are life lessons about preparedness or having a sense of humor—or preparedness *and* having a sense of humor, like the story of the Adirondack camping debacle of 2008. Some are "don't worry, the kids will turn out okay" reminders, like the story about the successful Wall Street finance wizard who, when he was 5, showed his best friend creative ways to pee in the back yard.

Stories teach the next generation the important lessons that anchor their lives in a time, place, and family. They connect the young, the old, and the middle-aged. But more important, they remind us to keep perspective, and to keep our eyes open for new material.

Everything, even—or especially—the major inconveniences and funny mistakes, provides the fabric of a new story. Times of endurance can be lightened by the mileage you'll get out of the story later on. (I told this to the girls as we huddled in that nylon tent by Eighth Lake as the rain poured down in 40-degree weather and the bears (probably) wandered hungrily outside: What a STORY this will make. Just wait till we tell Daddy! They glared at me.)

We humans live, work, and think in stories. You're writing one right now. Make it memorable.

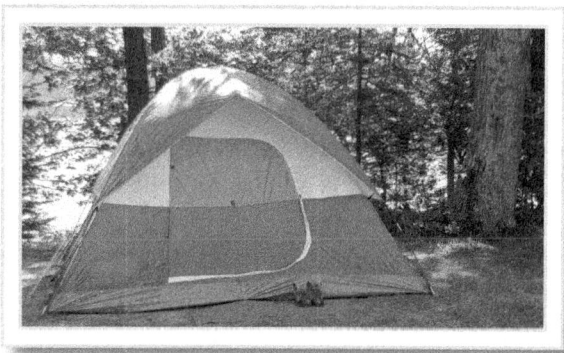

Photo: Julia Freeman-Woolpert

Creative Ways Kids Can Help Those in Need

Every year, starting around the middle of November, I get requests from families wanting to know ways that their family—kids emphatically included—can give to others less fortunate than themselves in their local community during the holidays. Including the kids, though...that can be the tough part. See, what a lot of folks have in mind is volunteering at soup kitchens, shelters, and the like. But most of these places exclude kids because of the potential liability involved in supervising them, even if their parents are present.

That's why my best answer is also one that, I think, benefits everyone: Many local organizations that assist those who are ill, lonely, or in bad financial straits have definite needs that the community— kids emphatically included!—can supply. The idea is to encourage kids to be entrepreneurial about researching these needs during the holidays (and all year round) and finding creative ways that they and their friends can be part of the solution. Kids, as easily as (and sometimes more effectively than) adults can organize food drives, clothing drives, toy drives, or drives to support pet shelters. It's really as easy as picking a meaningful cause or beneficiary, calling them to find out what they need, and then brainstorming ways to make it happen. Sometimes kids can contact local businesses for donations, or ask their friends for gently-used (or new) toys and books, or have a sale to raise money.

In Rochester, for example, enterprising young members of the Kids Coalition raised funds for those affected by Hurricane Sandy in 2012: One Sunday they organized SAND-AID: You ordered a breakfast bundle (bagels, cream cheese, a fruit, a drink, and a newspaper) for $15 and picked it up from a local store (or you could have it delivered for $20!). (See? If your kids were wondering how your family might help, all you had to do was eat breakfast!)

What a lot of kids in Rochester do is organize a toy drive for the Pirate Toy Fund. Their drive is all throughout December, but their big "push week" is the first week of December at the malls and at a supermarket called Wegmans. You drop off a new, unwrapped toy so that a needy child in our area can benefit at the holidays, and through the year.

And one of the most amazing things about encouraging your kids to help others in need, especially if it's a shared family experience, is that it will give your child the gift of a memory they'll remember long into the future.

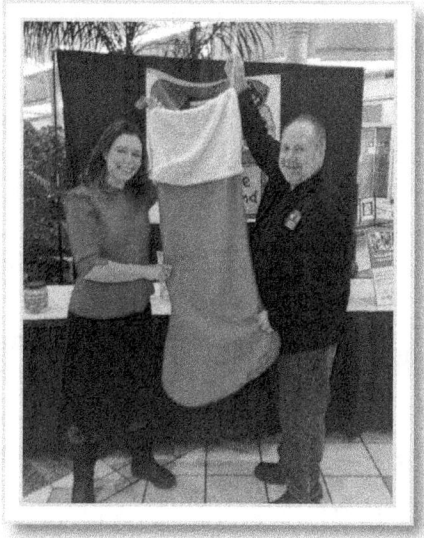

Photo: Dan Agnew

It Is Easier to Destroy Than to Build

It is infinitely easier, and faster, to destroy than to build. In Newtown, Connecticut on December 14, 2013, we saw how preciously few seconds it took someone to take 28 lives and shatter the sense of safety of millions.

For most families, that tragedy set in motion the action of considering what we can do to help our kids and our communities become strong and healthy. This requires becoming people who celebrate those who build, and by helping our kids see themselves as creators of good and important things.

...we're all standing on the shoulders of giants: the men and women who came before us who used their minds to invent what we now take for granted.

It's probably comfortably warm where you are right now, and you're probably not noticeably hungry. You may be reading through glasses or contact lenses. You're reading this on your computer, or on your phone, or on your tablet or in a printed book. Maybe you or one of your children wouldn't be alive were it not for modern medicine. This is all possible because we're all standing on the shoulders of giants: the men and women who came before us who used their minds to invent what we now take for granted. They were creators, not destroyers. That's who I want to be: someone who builds. And part of my job as a parent is to inspire my kids to be builders, too.

The Winter Solstice is right around the corner, and every year, my family celebrates an unusual tradition that I started in 1996 back when my husband and I were first married: We celebrate Lightbulb Day: On the "darkest evening of the year," the day we symbolically most need technology, we celebrate those who have made possible the relative comfort and safety and prosperity and happiness that we enjoy in this corner of the world. I invented a bunch of traditions (read them at www.kidsoutandabout.com/content/lightbulb-day-winter-solstice-celebration) that we continued even after we had our own kids.

We need to value, and foster, the idea of becoming people who build. Even if you don't do the full-fledged fun celebration that my family does, I suggest raising a glass at dinner to the builders, those who came before us and who live among us now. Remind your kids that everyone can be a creator of something. Focus their attention on the value of what they're creating day by day, even if it's small. And get them excited about the possibilities for what they might create in the future.

Parent as Tour Guide, Child as Tour Guide

I like the "tour guide" metaphor. I like it a lot. You can tell, because I've mentioned it quite a few times in this book.

Each of the regions in KidsOutAndAbout.com's network has much to offer families who want to launch their kids on a great path to a happy, healthy, productive, and culturally literate life. Our job is to lay them all out for you in an easy-to-appreciate way. We're each region's happiest cheerleaders.

...much joy flows in families when we allow our children to be the tour guides....

The other side of our mission is to help nurture the audience for all of the cultural, artistic, and recreation organizations, to help them sustain what they do so that it is available for the next generation.

After writing the essay I included earlier in this book about magic tips to get kids excited about visiting an art museum, I realized that I actually have the "tour guide" approach in my parenting as well as with the web site. My conviction is that if I convey a sense of excitement to Madison and Ella as I point out all of the intriguing things in our world—about art and history, physical fitness and music, nature and literature, science, and all the rest—then they'll become people who participate in these activities and help preserve them for generations to come. So far, it seems to be working well.

But I also realized how much joy flows in families when we allow our children to be the tour guides—especially during the holidays. Sometimes we work so hard to create magic for our kids that the holidays can feel exhausting. We zoom from packed mall to holiday concert to light show. But if we slow down and let the kids be our tour guides, if we pay attention and see the holidays through their eyes, it is that much more rewarding for us. We delight in creating memories for our kids, but we don't need to create a blur of memories each December. So... DO get out and about, but make sure you stop to light some candles, smell some fir trees, and drink some hot cider. Or whatever kindles the magic for your child. Then let them take you on a tour of their world.

Peak Prizes

If you have been reading my essays for many years, you'll have noticed that much of what I write is a variation on one of two themes: Celebrate! and Be the Karma. This idea incorporates both.

"Accentuate The Positive" is an old Harold Arlen / Johnny Mercer song that I remember best as sung by Ella Fitzgerald. It's a cliché message, I know. But the holiday time of year is full of clichés, so I'm going to indulge in some myself.

Most of the hills and valleys of life only last for the blink of the eye, but they endure in our memories for the rest of our lives. So how we interpret them is what matters most. The most productive strategy really is—cliché alert!— to focus on the peaks, and reflect on the valleys to help you accentuate how high up the peaks are (and to remind you to avoid those valleys next time).

Peaks are easier to remember if you get recognition from others. So here is my recommendation for a great (and free!) way to celebrate the end of the year: Hand out PEAK PRIZES!

My favorite way to do this is to mail letters to the people at the local businesses who have made life easier, and do it with your kids, if possible. Who makes a difference to you? Your librarian? Your pediatrician? The Home Depot? (Don't ignore the big chains... people work at them, too!) Address it to the person in charge (call to find out the manager's name). It can be something simple, like this:

Dear Ms. Smith:
I wanted to take a few minutes to let you know how much your business has meant to us this year. Every time we arrive at ____, we are greeted like friends. Your team members, particularly____, have always been helpful, especially (__this memorable time____). We wish you a productive upcoming year!

Sincerely,
The Joneses

And... this is important... print it out, put it in an envelope, address it by hand, and mail it. Give these folks a prize to show around proudly to all of the employees, to hang up on their wall for the first quarter, to remind them of what they do well and reinforce that for everyone who works there.

Celebrate. Be the karma. Your kids will be watching.

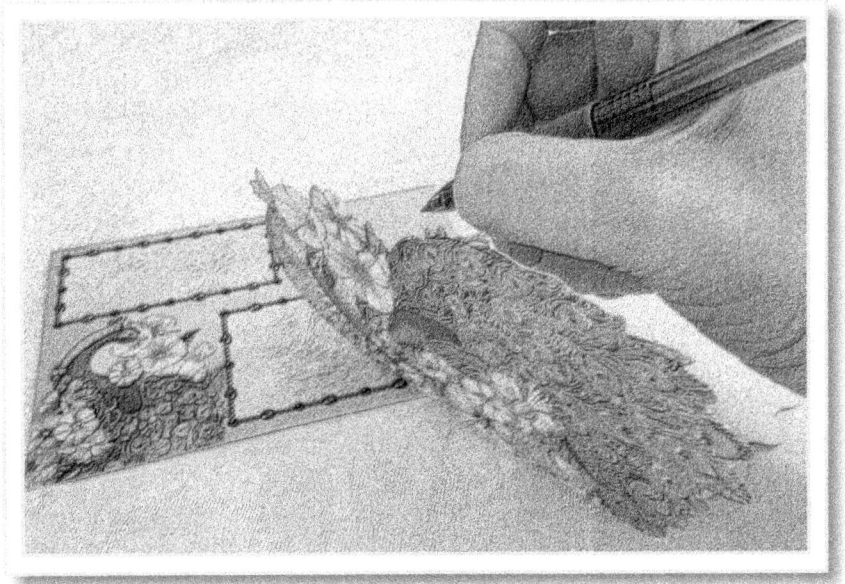

New Year's Wishes

Here are my New Year's wishes for you for the coming year:

More hugs and kisses

Fewer scrunchies and Legos on the floor

More pleases and thank yous

Fewer shouts of "Mine!"

More requests for green vegetables

Fewer time-outs

More days out the door with plenty of time to spare

Fewer days when bedtime can't come soon enough

More moments of wonder and discovery

And a nice vacation.

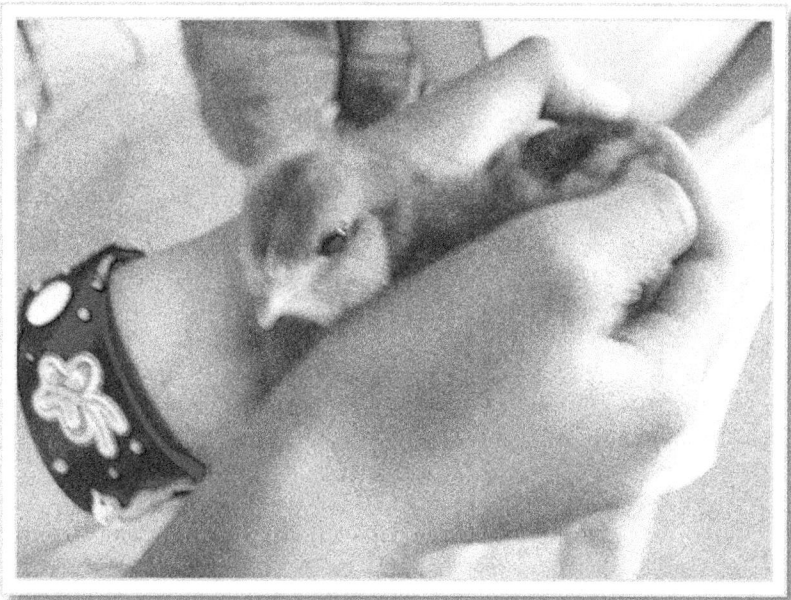

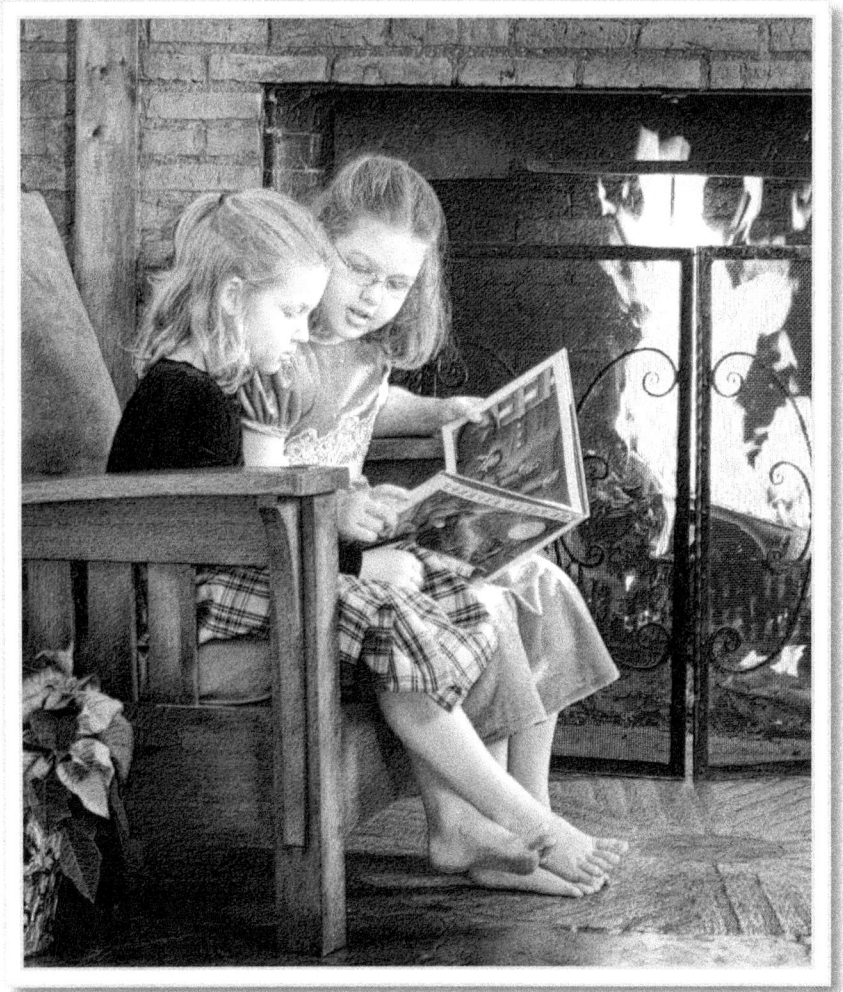

Photo: Honey DeLapa

Invitation to Be Part of Our Next Book

For one of our upcoming books, in addition to expanding on our own content, we'd like to hear from our readers! We know you have inspirational stories and advice, and we'd like to invite you to become a contributor. The book will focus on parenting inspiration, and our tentative chapter titles are listed below.

Book Chapters

- Be the Karma: Ways to encourage your child to build and contribute to the world
- It's All in the Family: Rituals, Traditions and Treasured Times: Ways to celebrate holidays, victories, vacations, etc.
- You Are Your Kid's Best Cheerleader: Ways to inspire, encourage and support your child to be his/her best self.
- Jumping the Hurdles: Challenging moments and how you, your child or your family overcame the problem.
- Housework, Habits, and Hobbies: Moving a child toward his or her future self.
- Mix it up: Anything that doesn't fall into the categories above.

We are looking for:

- Funny anecdotes
- Inspiring ideas
- Insightful or useful suggestions
- Touching, poignant or humorous stories

For more information or to contribute a piece, please visit **www.KidsOutAndAbout.com/InspireUs** to complete the form and upload your submission. All contributors whose work is accepted will receive a byline and a complimentary copy of the book.

Sincerely,
Deb and Carol

Seasons and Reasons

www.ingramcontent.com/pod-product-compliance
Lightning Source LLC
Chambersburg PA
CBHW071549040426
42452CB00008B/1119